EMPTY PROMISES

The Truth About You, Your Desires, and the Lies You're Believing

Pete Wilson

THOMAS NELSON

Since 1798

NASHVILLE   DALLAS   MEXICO CITY   RIO DE JANEIRO

Published in Nashville, Tennessee, by Thomas Nelson. Thomas Nelson is a registered trademark of Thomas Nelson, Inc.

Pete Wilson is represented by The A Group, a full service marketing, technology and brand development company in Brentwood, Tennessee. Learn more at www.AGroup.com.

Thomas Nelson, Inc., titles may be purchased in bulk for educational, business, fund-raising, or sales promotional use. For information, please e-mail SpecialMarkets@ ThomasNelson.com.

Unless otherwise noted, Scripture quotations are taken from the Holy Bible, New International Version®, NIV®. © 1973, 1978, 1984, 2011 by Biblica, Inc.™ Used by permission of Zondervan. All rights reserved worldwide. www.zondervan.com

Scripture quotations marked NKJV are from THE NEW KING JAMES VERSION®. © 1982 by Thomas Nelson, Inc. Used by permission. All rights reserved.

Scripture quotations marked NLT are from *Holy Bible*, New Living Translation. © 1996, 2004, 2007. Used by permission of Tyndale House Publishers, Inc., Wheaton, Illinois 60189. All rights reserved.

Library of Congress Cataloging-in-Publication Data

Wilson, Pete.
    Empty promises : the truth about you, your desires, and the lies you're believing / Pete Wilson.
        p. cm.
    Includes bibliographical references.
    ISBN 978-0-8499-4651-6 (trade paper)
    1. Christian life. 2. Truthfulness and falsehood—Religious aspects—Christianity. 3. Common fallacies. I. Title.
BV4501.3.W55625 2012
248.4—dc23   2011053187

Printed in the United States of America

12 13 14 15 16 QG 5 4 3

PRAISE FOR *EMPTY PROMISES*

"Pete Wilson is one of my favorite people and authors. If he writes it, I read it. Be prepared to think more deeply and live more authentically. This is not your average book—but rather a message which is compellingly real and relevant. Get your highlighter ready, this book is a game changer."

Jack Graham
Pastor of Prestonwood Baptist Church

"If you've ever gotten to the end of yourself–financially, physically, emotionally–and realized that you don't have all that you need to do all that God has called you to do, then you've come face-to-face with the empty promises of idolatry. Pete Wilson's book can help you. Through his integrity as a man of God, and his experience leading a high-impact, fast-paced church, he has unlocked some practical and challenging insights that will lead you to a deeper relationship with Christ."

Steven Furtick
Lead Pastor, Elevation Church
Author, *Sun Stand Still*

"I once heard it said that if nothing in this world can permanently satisfy us, then maybe we were created for something other than this world. I am so glad that Pete has decided to attack the idea of 'if I have *blank* then I will be happy,' because it doesn't work and in fact has left a trail of broken lives and disappointed people. Reality is that Jesus calls us away from certain things not because he is a cosmic killjoy but rather because he knows that nothing on this planet can bring permanent peace and satisfaction. This book isn't for those who want to be comfortable; it will attack some of the messages we are bombarded with every day in our culture. However, by digging into what Pete shows us the Scripture says about life, we can break free of the pursuit of meaningless things and focus our efforts on something that really does make an eternal impact."

Perry Noble
Senior Pastor, NewSpring Church

"Our human nature continually drives us to wanting 'more' out of life. Yet the journey to finding 'more' can often lead us down winding roads filled with distraction and, ultimately, destruction. Pastor Pete Wilson addresses these very issues in his new book, and I believe it will be a great encouragement to those who have found themselves on a pathway filled with empty promises. Pete's desire to see people flourish in their relationship with Christ is evident as he shares personal stories and lessons learned on his own journey of faith."

Brian Houston
Senior Pastor, Hillsong Church

"*Empty Promises* gives hope to those who need a jolt. It's a powerful reminder that God alone can fill your inner emptiness. Pete Wilson is the real deal. And this book is an essential tool for understanding the real you. We all long for something more in our lives. *Empty Promises* provides the framework to uncover God's best for us. God's first commandment to us regarding idols is brought to life in a practical way. A wake up call to our generation!"

Brad Lomenick
Executive Director, Catalyst

"Today's world is full of disappointed and discouraged people who've been chasing after all the wrong things. In *Empty Promises*, Pete points people toward their deepest longings of worth, significance, and love."

Jud Wilhite
Senior Pastor, Central Christian Church
Author, *Torn*

"One of the first lessons I learned in my marketing career was this: 'Everybody's insecure.' To leverage this, the suggested strategy in Marketing 101 was to position your product as a solution to your customers' insecurities. For decades now, this has proven to be a successful strategy. I would suggest there's a phrase for this approach. It's called *empty promises*. No wonder people in our society feel depleted, exhausted, and cheated.

"That's the bad news. The good news is that my friend Pete Wilson offers a different approach. Sure, we're all still insecure, but we don't have to fall for the same old lies and gimmicks. As Pete points out, we don't have to keep chasing 'more' because more never satisfies. Instead, there's a different road that leads to promises fulfilled. Pete helps lead us there through his authenticity, sharp writing, and wisdom. I highly encourage you to not only read *Empty Promises* but to also use it as small group curriculum. It's perfect for both.

"Pete Wilson is one of my favorite people. My prediction is that this will be one of your new favorite books. And that's no empty promise."

Jeff Henderson
Lead Pastor, Gwinnett Church

"Every human heart is looking for significance, worth, and value. In this book Pete Wilson helps us move beyond our endless pursuits of empty promises and helps us all discover and fulfill the deepest longings of our hearts."

Chris Hodges
Pastor, Church of the Highlands

To my three boys: J-man, Pooh Bear, and Boo-Boo,
three of the most amazing young men I've ever met.

I pray that one day this book might
serve as a road map for you.

When you're seduced by the empty promises of this world—
as we all are sometimes—I pray you live out Proverbs 24:16:

"The godly may trip seven times,
but they will get up again." (NLT)

May you always understand that Jesus offers you
what none of these counterfeit gods ever could.

He alone can fill your inner emptiness.

And he alone has the power to bring you, one
day, home where you belong—with him.

I love you with all my heart.

CONTENTS

ACKNOWLEDGMENTS

To Brandi . . . thanks for your constant love, friendship, and patience. Your belief in me allows me to chase after my dreams. I can't imagine sharing this journey with anyone but you!

To my Cross Point Church family . . . thank you for allowing me to serve you. Together we're creating an environment where it's okay to not be okay. It's sometimes messy, often not what we expected, and always more than we can do on our own. I love doing church and life with you guys.

To the Cross Point Staff team . . . nine years later it's still an honor to wake up every day and work with such an awesome group. You inspire me daily to be a better person. I love each and every one of you to death.

To Shannon Litton, Maurilio Amorim, and David Schroeder . . . thanks for your wisdom and faith not only to this book, but to me. Thanks for confronting and redeeming my desire to give up!

To Anne Christian Buchanan . . . as always, you challenge me to be a better writer. Thanks for your investment in this book.

To my entire team at Thomas Nelson: Matt Baugher, Debbie Wickwire, Emily Sweeney, Kristi Johnson, Stephanie Newton, Adria Haley, Tom Knight, and the entire amazing sales team, Caroline Green and Andrea Lucado . . . thank you guys for believing in me and giving me this incredible platform to share this message.

FOREWORD
BY RICK WARREN

Mother Teresa once observed that in India people are starv-ing physically, but in America people are starving spiritually and emotionally.

God wired each of us with a spiritual hunger that can only be satisfied by him. We use phrases like "There's got to be more to life than this," or "I'm bored . . . restless . . . empty . . . unfulfilled." Or even "I feel like something is missing in my life." Even when things are going well, there's always that little gnawing feeling on the inside. It is our *hunger* for God. We're made *by* God and *for* God, and until we understand that, life will never make sense. We make the mistake of looking for satisfaction in all the wrong places.

That's what this book is about. It uncovers the idols we create in our own hearts when we fail to look to God to meet our deepest needs. These idols of pleasure, prestige, passion, position, popularity, performance, and possessions inevitably betray us and let us down. They are, as my dear friend Pete Wilson says, "Empty Promises."

Too often we allow ourselves to be conned by "when and then" thinking. When I get married . . . when I make a lot of money . . . when I achieve a certain goal or status . . . THEN I'll be happy. But, as Solomon said, "No matter how much we see, we are never satisfied. No matter how much we hear, we are not content." (Ecclesiastes 1:8 NLT)

Advertising today is filled with empty promises that offer to fulfill our spiritual hunger. Products from coffee to cigarettes promise "satisfaction guaranteed" and "The taste that satisfies!" If that were true you'd only need one cup of coffee and never need another cigarette!

Without Christ, we tend to approach life like we do a late night refrigerator raid: We're restless and can't sleep so we get up and go to the refrigerator. We don't know what we want—we just know we are hungry. We open the door and stare, scanning the contents, hoping something will look good and catch our attention. Next, we start "grazing"—nibbling a little on this, then nibbling a little on that. But nothing tastes good. Nothing satisfies. We close the refrigerator door, and go back to bed *still hungry.* That scene describes the lives of most people.

Today there are more than twice as many products and services available as there were ten years ago, and most of them promise what they cannot deliver. But are people twice as happy as they were ten years ago? Of course not. One man admitted to me, "Even when I get what I want, it's not what I want! I'm still dissatisfied."

This book points you to the answer in your search for satisfaction and significance. It will change your life if you'll listen, learn, and apply the powerful truths it contains. Pete Wilson will help you recognize your *real* hunger and the *only* source for real satisfaction.

Psalm 37:4 says, "Take delight in the LORD, and he will give you your hearts desires." Don't seek happiness, seek God! The promise of happiness isn't contained in a product. That promise is found in a person—Jesus Christ. "For all of God's promises have been fulfilled in Christ with a resounding 'Yes!'" (2 Cor. 1:20). I invite you to begin the journey!

— Rick Warren
Pastor, Saddleback Church

CHAPTER ONE
DECEPTIVELY GOOD

I've been given an incredible gift.

In fact, I've actually been given 13,790 gifts. That's how many days of life I've been given to date.

Out of these thirteen-thousand-plus days I've been given, some have been challenging, some depressing, some adventurous. A few I wouldn't mind living over and over and over. I'm not sure I can actually pick an all-time favorite, but I sure have had some memorable ones.

There was the day I was born. That was a good day (I'm told).

The day I learned to walk was pretty good too.

The day I fell in love for the first time—who could ever forget that one?

The day I got my driver's license was definitely good for me. (I bet it was a scary day for my parents.)

The day I got married was a big one, and the days my wife, Brandi, gave birth to each of our three sons and I held them in my arms for the first time—unforgettable.

Then there are the days like one I experienced recently while on vacation with my family in Florida. Brandi and I sat on the beach with our feet in the sand, discussing our dreams for the future. With every word that came out of our mouths, we realized just how blessed we are. As we talked and dreamed together in the sun, we watched our three boys, who are now nine, six, and four, leaping over the ocean waves without a care in the world. A few hours later, we all sat on the beach together and watched that golden sun seem to drop into the ocean.

That day will be etched into my mind for a lifetime, not necessarily for what we did, but for how I felt. So many of my deep desires for purpose, worth, significance, acceptance, security, love, and beauty were met. For a brief few hours, it seemed like the perfect day.

Sadly, it didn't last.

Because right in there with those wonderful, good, blessed days, there have been plenty of days when I struggled with a nagging or even painful sense of wanting . . . more. When who I am and what I have just didn't seem like enough.

Do you ever feel that way? I believe we all do at one time or another. Some things just seem to be consistent among most people I encounter on this earth.

We enjoy how it feels when the wind blows across our faces.

We root for the underdog.

We love how it feels to win, and we don't like being told what to do.

We're awestruck when we see sights like the Grand Canyon, Niagara Falls, or a bright red tree in the middle of autumn.

We love hearing the laughter of a small child.

We are disgusted by the contents of a chicken nugget, but we still eat them once in a while. (Well, maybe that one is just me.)

And beyond that, I believe most of us have a deep longing to feel certain things.

Twenty-one days after you were conceived, a tiny little electrical impulse stimulated your heart muscle. It was so faint it could hardly be detected, but it was in fact the very first beat of your heart. From that moment, you've been on a journey, and there are certain things your soul longs for on this journey. Whether you've realized it or not, your life is shaped by your search for them. You're designed to throw your energy and your respect toward whatever you believe can provide you with what you desire:

- purpose
- worth
- significance
- acceptance
- security
- love
- beauty

This is true for every one of us. We all long for more of something in our lives. We all treasure something or someone above our everyday experience. We all give our devotion to somebody or something. These impulses are a part of our DNAs, etched in our natures, as normal and natural as breathing. I believe they have been placed inside our souls by our Creator God.

Simply put, we are a people wired to worship. The question isn't, "Do we worship?" The question is, "Who (or what) do we worship?"

I believe the yearning for more that haunts us all exists to ultimately lead us to the person of Jesus Christ. That drive to worship is designed to impel us into proper relationship with the One who can fulfill our deepest desires.

This is showing my cards a bit early, but I'm convinced that only through Jesus will we ultimately discover our souls' contentment. Yes, we may encounter good days or even the occasional perfect day. But our longing souls will never discover true satisfaction until we turn to him. And whenever we attempt to find fulfillment elsewhere, we open ourselves up to a world of futility and frustration.

THE IDOL FACTORY

On my first trip to Kolkata, India, I visited a temple called the Kali Temple. Thousands of Hindus in Kolkata line up every day to pray to the goddess Kali. They worship her, hoping to gain power, victory, and healing in certain areas of their lives.

Some of the ways they worship astounded me. Not that many years ago, child sacrifices were common. Today, a hundred to a hundred fifty goats are sacrificed daily at the Kali Temple. A pool just outside the temple is believed to have healing powers. People pay to have their families and friends lowered into the murky, stagnant waters. There is also a tree with red ribbons hanging all over it. When I asked about the tree, I learned that women pay money to buy these red strings and then tie them to the tree, praying that Kali will allow them to have children.

I walked away with a supreme sense of sadness and darkness. How could a group of people be lured into such a ridiculous lie? How could they not see that this was just an elaborate money-making scheme for a handful of greedy priests?

But do you know what is equally ridiculous? You and I believing that a little more money is going to make us happy. You and I believing that moving up one more position at work is going to give us value. You and I believing that if we could just get a particular person to love us, we would have security.

Idols, in other words, aren't found just in pagan temples.

You see, I'm not really concerned that we are going to worship a tree. The real problem in our culture is not the making of physical idols—what some call external idolatry. What we have to guard against in our culture is internal idolatry. Ezekiel 14:3 describes this: "These men have set up idols in their hearts."

What is an idol? Traditionally we define it as anything that is more important to us than God. But I find that people shrug that definition off too readily. It's easy to fool ourselves into thinking that nothing is more important to us than God.

So let's define it like this: idolatry is when I look to something that does not have God's power to give me what only God has the power and authority to give.

> So let's define it like this: idolatry is when I look to something that does not have God's power to give me what only God has the power and authority to give.

It's when we take good things like a successful career, love, material possessions, even family, and turn to them in the hope that they'll provide what only God can provide.

It's when we buy into the empty promise that such things can give us the significance, security, safety, and fulfillment we crave.

It's when we feel a God-given appetite and try to fill it with something that isn't God.

John Calvin famously said, "The human heart is a perpetual factory of idols."[1] I agree. When I look back on my own life, I see a distinct pattern of depending on trivial things to give me what only God can give me. And the results aren't pretty.

If I'm really honest with you, there are nights after the lights go out and the noise in my life dissipates that I lie there in bed acutely aware of an inner emptiness. And while I have moments and even days of what seem to be deep satisfaction or soothing peace, those feelings evaporate quickly. I run and run after them, but they seem as fleeting as a disappearing sun, and then once again that gnawing inner emptiness is back.

Have you felt it too—that unquenchable longing that tempts you to sacrifice everything you have and everything you are to be a little more beautiful, a little richer, a little more powerful and successful, a little more secure or in control, a little more loved—all in this futile attempt to heal the inner emptiness? It's so easy to fall into the trap of "if only":

- If I owned this, I would feel worthy.
- If I achieved that, I would feel significant.
- If I had what they have, I would be content.
- If I made a little more money, I would finally be satisfied.
- If I got that promotion, I would feel valued.
- If I could only get that person to love me, I would have security.

But sooner or later we discover the heartbreaking truth that no matter how beautiful or rich or powerful we become, it's never enough.

C. S. Lewis wrote,

> Most people, if they had really learned to look into their own hearts, would know that they do want, and want acutely, something that cannot be had in this world. There are all sorts of things in this world that offer to give it to you, but they never quite keep their promise.[2]

We can sacrifice everything for these promises, but they will just leave us wanting, longing, used, and empty. We'll never find what we need in an idol.

Unfortunately, that doesn't stop us from trying.

THE WAITING ROOMS OF LIFE

Scripture is full of examples of our constant need to grab at almost anything to try and fill our deep, built-in longings for worth, significance, acceptance, love, and beauty. One of the first and greatest examples is found in Exodus 32.

At this point, God had just set his chosen people, the Israelites, free from over four hundred years of captivity to the Egyptians. They were finally on their way to living the life God had designed for them to live. But there was a problem. Things weren't moving as fast as they would've liked, and they were getting restless. Their leader, Moses, was absent, and their impatience drove them to take things into their own hands.

> When the people saw that Moses was so long in coming down
> from the mountain [Moses was on Mt. Sinai for nearly six weeks],
> they gathered around Aaron and said, "Come, make us gods who
> will go before us. As for this fellow Moses who brought us up out
> of Egypt, we don't know what has happened to him." (v. 1)

I think it's important to point out the catalyst for what happened next. The instigating factor was having to wait.

Don't you hate waiting? Most of us do. Waiting has never been a popular pastime, and our culture makes it worse. We live in a day of fast this and instant that, and having to wait for anything is a big frustration. We've started to believe that faster is always better. We've become seduced by such words as *instant* and *easy*. We've become quickaholics, dependent on getting what we want when we want it.

Why do we hate waiting so much? There are many reasons, but I think one of the biggest is that waiting makes us feel helpless and powerless. Lewis Smedes described it like this: "As creatures who cannot by themselves bring about what they hope for, we wait in darkness for a flame we cannot light. We wait in fear for a happy ending that we cannot write. We wait for a 'not yet' that feels like a 'not ever.'"[3]

As you probably know, Moses was away receiving the Ten Commandments from God. Apparently, he was away much longer than the children of Israel expected him to be. They were feeling frustrated, vulnerable, and helpless in the wilderness. So in his absence, they decided they wanted a different god to worship.

When you think about it, it's amazing how quickly this idol response set in. Just three months before, God had delivered them from four hundred years of captivity. He had provided

- freedom when they were captive;
- deliverance when they were pursued;
- food (manna) when they were hungry;
- water (from a rock) when they were thirsty;
- guidance from a cloud during the day;
- guidance from a pillar of fire at night.

And it wasn't enough. None of it was enough for them to continue worshipping the God who had done all this. Instead, they decided to build an idol, a golden calf, and worship the calf instead.

Why did they do this? I suspect it was because God was making them wait, and the children of Israel couldn't stand the waiting. This is important to note because, apparently, when the need for hurry meets the desire for control, it becomes really easy to start worshipping someone and something other than our Creator God.

Aaron answered them, "Take off the gold earrings that your wives, your sons and your daughters are wearing, and bring them to me." So all the people took off their earrings and brought them to Aaron. He took what they handed him and made it into an idol cast in the shape of a calf, fashioning it with a tool. Then they said, "These are your gods, Israel, who brought you up out of Egypt." (vv. 2–4)

When Moses walked down from Mount Sinai with the Ten Commandments and saw what was happening, he became so furious that he tossed the two tablets that God had just etched on his behalf off the side of the mountain.

As I'm sure you can remember, the very first commandment was, "You shall have no other gods before me" (Ex. 20:3).

The very first law of the most famous moral code in the history of the world has to do with the trap of idolatry. God warns his people not to worship other gods. Don't expect anything other than God to give what only God can give.

Why such prominence for this command? I think it's because God knew something not only about the children of Israel but about me and about you.

He knows about the inner emptiness inside of us. He knows about that ache that haunts every one of us. He knows this longing for purpose, worth, significance, acceptance, security, love, and beauty pulsates through our veins, and we will stop at nothing (including building our own golden calves) to fulfill those longings.

He knows, remember, because he put those longings there to direct us to him. And he gave us that commandment to spare us from the heartache of empty promises.

Furthermore, I think this commandment had prominence because it's almost impossible for us to follow and obey the other nine if we break this first one.

"You shall have no other gods before me."

Just think about it: your response to those eight words influences every facet of your life. Idolatry isn't simply a sin. It's what is fundamentally wrong with the human heart.

DEPLETED

I've made it a practice to look into others' eyes. The person who passes me in the grocery story aisle, the person behind the counter at the gas station, the person who rushes by me on the street.

Do you know what I see most often? Is it life, joy, love, vibrancy? No, most often what I see is exhaustion.

Just look at the people around you, the people you live with, work with, or do life with. You'll see it too. They're exhausted, depleted, lacking. They may look like they have it all together, but under it all they're falling apart.

The church I've been blessed to pastor for the past nine years includes plenty of singles. I was never really a single adult. I started dating Brandi when I was nineteen, and we were married at twenty-one. So I basically transitioned from being a teenager to being married.

But having spent a lot of time with single adults, I know they face a tremendous amount of pressure.

> Idolatry isn't simply a sin. It's what is fundamentally wrong with the human heart.

I recently began meeting with a young woman by the name of Kara who is fairly involved with our church. I don't know her exact age, but I would guess she's about twenty-seven. And when she showed up for our first appointment, it was instantly clear to me that she had been through some kind of hell. You could see the pain on her face.

Kara started telling me that a guy she had been dating for the past few months had just called things off with her. She was distraught about their breakup. Through her tears she just kept saying, "I'm so tired of this. I'm so tired of this. Why can't I find someone to care for me? Why can't I find a relationship like everyone else? Why do I keep making the same mistakes over and over? I'm so tired of this."

Over several appointments together, we started to talk a little more in depth about why Kara felt she needed a man. It wasn't just that she was lonely. To her, having a boyfriend gave her not only a sense of worth but also a certain status. It made her feel like somebody. The trouble was, Kara couldn't seem to find what she wanted so desperately.

Over the past two years, she had been through no fewer than a dozen guys. None of these relationships had worked out the way she desired, despite her attempts to become everything those men wanted her to become. She dressed to please them, arranged her schedule around them, deferred to their wishes. She also had sex with most of these men, which only made her feel more used, guilty, and betrayed.

I remember looking at her at one point and saying, "Kara, I don't think you were designed to give yourself away the way you do. And while you were designed for community and companionship—we all are—I don't think you were designed to find your purpose and worth in some guy. There may be numerous reasons you don't feel like you're thriving right now in your life, but have you considered your real problem might be idolatry—that you're looking to a man to give you what only God can give you?"

It's no surprise that Kara was feeling exhausted. Because that's the thing about idolatry—it will plumb wear you out. Idols don't have the capacity to breathe life back into you, so all they do is take and take and take.

In the same way the women in India were giving what little money they had in hope of getting pregnant, only to be left feeling robbed, you're going to give of your money, your time and your energies, your heart and your passions, hoping one of your idols may finally deliver.

But since idolatry is expecting something other than God to give you what only God can give, you end up having to depend on yourself and your own efforts to produce something only God can produce. In essence, you're playing God, and that's exhausting.

To further complicate the issue, so many of the idols—the empty promises—in our culture today involve performance. Performance is also very exhausting. Think about your own life. Are you tired of

- trying to keep the perfect house?
- striving to have the perfect marriage?
- looking like you have it all together?
- feeling the pressure to look like you just walked out of a magazine?
- struggling to raise perfect kids who excel academically and socially and can crush a T-ball over the fence?
- working to make more money than everyone else in your circle?
- attempting to climb the ladder faster than the guy who's right on your heels?

Are you weary of all the empty promises that leave you longing and aching for more? This performance-driven lifestyle is just another form of *idolatry*, and it will eventually leave you exhausted, bitter, and ready to give up.

But I want you to read these powerful and healing words of Jesus. As your eyes scan them, I pray your heart will absorb them. Jesus said,

> Come to me, all you who are weary and burdened, and I will give you rest. Take my yoke upon you and learn from me, for I am gentle and humble in heart, and you will find rest for your souls. For my yoke is easy and my burden is light. (Matt. 11:28–30)

Are you tired of striving?
Tired of performing?
Tired of trying to be someone you're not?

What if there were another way? A way that gives life instead of inducing stress?

You see, I believe that God has not given up on you. He is, in fact, powerfully present in your life, even if he seems to be absent. He has revealed himself through a man, Jesus, who came to earth to show us how to live and then died for our sins. In his resurrection, he gave us hope that we can indeed experience the fulfillment of our desires.

Jesus is continually inviting people to give up their idols and follow him. Jesus, and Jesus alone, is worthy of our whole devotion. He alone has the authority to forgive all of our sins. He alone has the wisdom to guide our whole lives. He alone leaves us invigorated rather than exhausted, at peace rather than anxious. He alone has the power to fill the gnawing inner emptiness we all experience and bring purpose to each and every day that he sees fit to grant us as a gift.

CHAPTER TWO
THE AWARE LIFE

Lindsey is a strong woman who always seems to have a lot going for her—a great family, a good job, and a host of supportive and caring people God has placed in her life. She's been a family friend for almost a decade.

On an unusually cold and windy March day, I met Lindsey for coffee. I had asked her to meet me because I was a bit worried about her. Call it pastoral instinct or just a gut feeling, but when I ran into her at church the Sunday before, I could tell something just wasn't quite right. That's one of the beauties and sometimes annoying realities of having longtime friends around. They pick up on things an average acquaintance never would.

As we sat down at the local coffee shop, I gave Lindsey the standard, "You don't have to talk if you don't want to, but I just wanted to check on you. Everything all right?" And that was all I needed to say. Before I took my first sip of coffee, she was pouring out her heart. It was almost as if she had all these emotions boiling under the surface and she had been dying for someone to finally ask her.

"I don't know what's going on, Pete," she told me. "At first I thought it was depression and then maybe a midlife crisis, but I just feel this sense of unhappiness. I spent the first twenty years of my life dreaming of what I thought I wanted in life, and I spent the next twenty years making that dream a reality. I've got the marriage and family I thought I wanted and the house I thought I wanted and the career I thought I wanted. I've got it all, but none of it has met the expectations I'd built up. I thought achieving these things would fulfill me. So I've been running and running and running, trying to achieve my goals. But now that I've met them, I feel like I need to keep running because there's no satisfaction. I just don't know what the point of it all is anymore."

I wish I could say this was the first time I had heard words like these, but it wasn't. Hardly a week goes by that I don't hear these same sentiments shared over and over.

I spent the next hour and a half trying to help Lindsey look behind the curtain of her life. Like so many of us, she'd just been going through the motions, chasing after what she thought would eventually give her meaning and purpose and satisfaction. What she needed to do was pause and begin to examine *why* she was chasing the things she was chasing.

LURKING BELOW THE SURFACE

You see, the question we're dealing with in this book is not "Do you have idols?" We've already determined that the heart is an idol factory. The real question for any of us is this: Which idol is God's biggest rival in your life?

Several years ago I found myself in a situation not that unlike Lindsey's. I guess if I'm honest, I've been there several times over the course of my adult life. In this particular instance I discovered

I'd been deceiving myself in a number of ways, convincing myself I could find self-worth from several empty promises.

In an effort to find out why I felt so empty, I started to pay more attention to what was going on internally. Paying attention or examining my life forces me to face the internal questions I can no longer keep quiet. I was compelled to come face-to-face with what was lurking at the deepest level of my soul.

These were questions I could no longer ignore:

- Why do I continue to say yes to others, even though I'm overextended and hurting those closest to me?
- Why do I continue to struggle with showing my wife love on a more consistent basis, the way I should?
- Why are my emotions affected more by how many people show up at church than by just being in the presence of our caring God?
- Why do I continue to strive to find my identity in things like acceptance, power, and money instead of in who God says I am?

Each and every question that came to my mind revealed another level of self-deception in my life. It revealed another empty promise I was chasing after.

The Bible speaks quite frequently on this idea of self-deception. Obadiah 1:3 says, for example, "The pride of your heart has deceived you." And Proverbs 14:12 warns,

> There is a way that appears to be right,
> but in the end it leads to death.

The bottom line is that every single human being has an unbelievable capacity for self-deception. It's no wonder we fall for

> The bottom line is that every single human being has an unbelievable capacity for self-deception. It's no wonder we fall for these empty promises over and over and over.

these empty promises over and over and over.

The other day I was arguing with my nine-year-old son, who wanted to go outside in the middle of winter wearing a T-shirt and shorts. I said to him, "Jett, you're going to freeze out there. Go put some clothes on."

He responded, "Dad, it's not that cold."

"Yes, it is, buddy. I've been out this morning, and it's literally freezing outside."

We argued back and forth a few times, and then I said, "Son, remember the other day when you went out to play football but you came in because you were so miserably cold? It's that cold outside today."

Despite my clear warnings and his recent history, Jett opted to go outside wearing next to nothing. Ten minutes hadn't passed when I heard him fling open the front door and come running inside.

I said, "What's up, buddy?"

As he continued to run up the stairs he said, "I'm going to get some clothes on. It's freezing outside."

I had to laugh. It's that kind of self-deception that has gotten me in trouble with empty promises over and over again.

Despite the wisdom of God's Word.

Despite what friends might be warning me about.

Despite my painful history.

I somehow convince myself that *this* time I'll find purpose if I get a little more power, or I'll find significance if I become a little more popular.

HELP ME KNOW ME

Knowing our capacity for self-deception, how do we make sure that we're not regularly falling into that trap? People will often point to Psalm 139:23–24 to illustrate the need for self-examination. It says,

> Search me, God, and know my heart;
> test me and know my anxious thoughts.
> See if there is any offensive way in me,
> and lead me in the way everlasting.

But if you back up to the beginning of Psalm 139 you'll discover something interesting. The psalm actually begins by acknowledging that God has *already* searched us:

> You have searched me, LORD,
> and you know me. (v. 1)

Ruth Haley Barton said this verse "may point to the fact that the real issue in self-examination is not that I am inviting God to know me (since he already does) but that I am inviting God to *help me know me*."[1]

As I've been spending more and more time alone with God, trying to get to the bottom of the empty promises I've bought into, I've started praying, "God, help me to know me. Help me tear down the scaffolding of power, praise, perfectionism, and performance that I use to prop myself up. Strengthen me so I can bear to be naked and vulnerable in your presence, willing to see the areas of my life where Christlikeness is so lacking."

"Willing to see"—that's crucial. Because most of us are experts at hiding from what we don't want to know about our own lives.

When my middle son, Gage, was just a toddler, he loved to play hide-and-seek. He especially loved the hiding part, so typically I would have to be "it." After sticking my face in my hands and counting to twenty, I would search the house for him, announcing out loud each step I took and each place I looked. Whenever I found him hiding behind the couch or underneath the table, he would quickly close his eyes as tightly as he could, convinced that if he couldn't see me, I wouldn't be able to see him.

Often we play a similar game with God. In our adult version of hide-and-seek, we hide behind all kinds of noise and distractions. We get up in the morning and turn on the TV, hoping it will distract us from having to think. We'll get in the car and immediately turn on the radio or jump on the phone. Our days will be full of surface-level, meaningless conversations about the weather, politics, or the latest celebrity gossip.

> The truth is, all the money, talent, attractiveness, and popularity in the world will not protect anyone from the stupidity of sin. And none of those things will fulfill the burning desire for more that drives people to fall for false promises.

We actually fool ourselves into thinking that if we don't acknowledge the areas of our lives where we've bought into empty promises, maybe God won't notice them either. We all desperately need to open our eyes. We're not fooling anyone. And while self-awareness can be painful, it can also be the beginning of transformation.

What would you answer if I were to ask what's most important to you? A lot of people I know would reply without thinking: "My relationship with Jesus." They'd insist that God is at the very center of their lives. However, careful self-examination may uncover something quite different.

Will you take a few minutes to live with the following questions?

I think they'll begin to uncover some of the hidden idols you may have in your life. Honestly ask yourself:

- What occupies my mind? What do I spend time daydreaming about?
- Who or what do I tend to be jealous of?
- What do I spend most of my time doing?
- Where does the majority of my money go?

What you'll quickly discover—as I have—is that it's easy for our hearts to wander away from Jesus and toward other people or things, thinking they'll give us what only he can give us.

THE PURSUIT

I'll never forget the long summer day between my sophomore and junior year of college. It started like any normal day. Brandi and I had been dating a little over a year, and we were babysitting her little cousins, who were in town.

The news reports had been floating around for days that legendary NFL running back and movie star O. J. Simpson was a possible suspect in the killing of his ex-wife. Then the event happened that caught the nation's attention—O. J. driving down the interstate in that infamous white Bronco with dozens of Los Angeles policemen in pursuit.

Brandi and I sat there in shock as we watched this entire event unfolding on national television. I remember just shaking my head and thinking, *No way*. How could this guy be so stupid? He's got money, fame, and just about anything else a person could want. How could he spiral down like this?

And it wasn't just O. J. Like most people, I'll never forget where I was and what I was doing when news broke about Princess Diana's fatal car wreck, John F. Kennedy Jr.'s plane crash, Michael Jackson's overdose, or the public unraveling of Tiger Woods's and Arnold Schwarzenegger's marriages. Each of these events had me glued to the television as I watched the reports unfold. And I wasn't alone. The whole country, it seemed, was fascinated.

There are probably a variety of deep psychological reasons events like these capture our attention, but surely one major theme is that these folks seemed to have it all—money, achievement, possessions, fame, power. Surely those awful things couldn't be happening to *them*. And surely, if we were in their shoes, we wouldn't mess things up the way they did.

The truth is, all the money, talent, attractiveness, and popularity in the world will not protect anyone from the stupidity of sin. And none of those things will fulfill the burning desire for more that drives people to fall for false promises.

Dallas Willard said that one of the fundamental questions every human being asks is, "Who has 'the good life'?"[2] I believe our endless and growing preoccupation with celebrities has to do largely with that question.

In my own life I have to consider this question: Why am I so interested in what Tiger Woods does not only on the golf course but also in his personal life? Why am I drawn to pick up *People* or watch *E!* for the latest celebrity gossip? I think I'm drawn to that type of information because there is a part of me that thinks those people are enjoying the life I've always wanted. The life that part of me believes is the good life.

Was I born with the desire to have that kind of lifestyle? Of course not. My visions of living like the rich and famous have been formed in me over time, shaped by the culture I live in. Media and advertising have defined the good life in terms of access to nice cars, big homes, great bodies, overinflated fame, total independence, and a huge following. And even though on some level I know better, I still find it hard to escape those messages that have bombarded me, especially when I'm watching coverage of the rich and famous at play.

Surely that's true of most of us. At some level we're convinced that celebrities are the ones who have the good life. And we are fascinated, maybe even drawn to them because they live a life we can't help wanting. In a way, celebrities are our new gods. We like to fantasize that our lives could become like theirs—and then we, too, would be beautiful, desirable, talented, and crazy rich. And while we may live in the tension between our desire to have those things and our desire to be good people, inevitably we will pursue a life that we think is desirable. We will pursue what we determine in our minds to be the good life.

The problem is that when we actually catch up and achieve this so-called good life, we discover—as so many celebrities have discovered—that it's nothing more than empty promises that, at best, leave us wanting more.

THE ANT TRAP

As I write this, I'm watching a trail of ants march under my desk. Over the past few days, these pesky creatures have invaded our house. I don't know why, but ants drive me crazy.

Upon noticing their arrival, Brandi suggested we call an exterminator. That sounded good to me until I realized how much it would cost to have someone come out and take care of our ant problem. So in true male fashion, I promised her I would come up with a solution.

A trip to the local hardware store equipped me with an amazing product. The directions seemed simple enough. All I had to do was squirt some gel on a small piece of cardboard and then place it where I'd seen the ants. The gel contains something that attracts the ants; the ants eat the gel and then take it back to their nest to offer their friends. And while the gel tastes good to the ants, it also poisons them.

I'm currently watching hundreds and hundreds of ants lining up in single file across the floor of my house. The little guys are climbing on top of each other to get to this delicious, poisonous stuff. It's amazing to watch. They have no idea that their pursuit will lead to their demise.

What an amazing picture this is of how many of us live in today's culture. We're lining up by the thousands to pursue what we've been convinced is the good life. And while the very thing we chase looks good or feels good or tastes good, it's also poison to our souls.

What's the alternative? One possibility, I suppose, is to rid ourselves of our desires. That is a foundational principle of Buddhism—to attempt to reach a point where you simply don't desire anything. But while I believe our desires can make us sick and that getting what we think we want can be bad for us, the idea of eliminating desire is problematic for me.

Why? First of all, I think it's impossible. Many of these desires are hardwired within me; I couldn't get rid of them even if I wanted to. But more important, as I've mentioned, I believe our desires are inside us for a reason. True, if left unmonitored, they can lead us right into empty promises. But they are ultimately there to lead us to Christ, the only person who can actually fulfill them. As C. S. Lewis wrote,

> If we consider the unblushing promises of reward and the staggering nature of the rewards promised in the Gospels, it would seem that Our Lord finds our desires not too strong, but too weak. We are half-hearted creatures, fooling about with drink and sex and ambition when infinite joy is offered us, like an ignorant child who wants to go on making mud pies in a slum because he cannot

imagine what is meant by the offer of a holiday at sea. We are far too easily pleased.[3]

Often, what we think is the good life is not really the good life at all. It's nothing but smoke and mirrors. It's an illusion, an elaborate trap. It's a collection of empty promises. But that doesn't mean the good life doesn't exist. It simply means we need to open ourselves to what the good life really is—a life than is far sweeter and more satisfying than anything we can even imagine. That's the good life that "God has prepared for those who love him" (1 Cor. 2:9). The good life that requires us to listen deeply for what we really want and to look beyond empty promises to the One who can fulfill our deepest desires.

> I believe our desires are inside us for a reason. True, if left unmonitored, they can lead us right into empty promises. But they are ultimately there to lead us to Christ, the only person who can actually fulfill them.

I'm praying this book will serve as sort of an invitation for you to look deeper into your own life. I pray you'll do exactly what I invited my friend Lindsey to do that day in the coffee shop. I invited her to start paying attention to her life. I asked her to wake up and look deep into her soul to uncover the layers upon layers of self-deception and the truth that lies beneath them.

That's what I'm challenging you to do too—to learn to be aware of

- what you're saying;
- what you're doing;
- what you're thinking;
- how you're acting;

- where you're coming from;
- what your motives are.

If you're not, you'll spend your life trying to find your identity and worth in the empty promises of attractiveness, acceptance, wealth, and power.

But they'll just leave you empty and wanting more.

CHAPTER THREE
THE SEDUCTION OF ACHIEVEMENT

About six months ago I had a wake-up call. I was sitting at the desk in my home office with my head in my hands weeping uncontrollably. I had just finished responding to a barrage of e-mails that had once again filled up my mailbox. Looking at the next three weeks in my Outlook calendar had left me with severe chest pain. The pressure of my hectic professional life had finally caught up with me—all the

- message preparation;
- blogging;
- book writing;
- traveling;
- leadership demands;
- pastoral counseling.

I've never had a panic attack, but for the first time in my life I felt like I was having one, and it scared me to death.

I sat there on that Saturday morning praying my family would not wake up and come downstairs to see me like that. I prayed and confessed to God that I couldn't live like that anymore. Something had to give.

Without even realizing it I had become addicted to an increasingly dangerous drug in my life.

The drug of public productivity.

I picked up that phrase from a letter I read immediately following my meltdown. A well-known, well-respected pastor confessed to his church community:

> I see several species of pride in my soul that, while they may not rise to the level of disqualifying me for ministry, grieve me, and have taken a toll on my relationship with Liz and others who are dear to me. How do I apologize to you, not for a specific deed, but for ongoing character flaws, and their effects on everybody? I'll say it now, and no doubt will say it again, I'm sorry. Since I don't have just one deed to point to, I simply ask for a spirit of forgiveness; and I give you as much assurance as I can that I am not making peace, but war, with my own sins.
>
> Liz and I are rock solid in our commitment to each other, and there is no whiff of unfaithfulness on either side. But, as I told the elders, "rock solid" is not always an emotionally satisfying metaphor, especially to a woman. A rock is not the best image of a woman's tender companion. In other words, the precious garden of my home needs tending. I want to say to Liz that she is precious to me in a way that, at this point in our 41-year pilgrimage, can be said best by stepping back for a season from virtually all public commitments.[1]

But it was another sentence in that letter that really got to me. He wrote: "In thirty years, I have never let go of the passion for public productivity."

I got a bit of a sick feeling in the pit of my stomach when I read those words, because in many ways they describe me.

Driven to succeed.

Focused on achievement.

Determined to be known as a person who makes a difference.

Dependent on that heady feeling that I'm doing something important . . . no matter what the cost.

In too many ways, in different seasons of my life, I've put building a great church ahead of investing in my family and taking care of my own health. I've put answering all of my e-mails ahead of spending time with God. I've made delivering a strong message more important than submitting to the Lord and letting him actually change me.

Why do I do it? Like any addict, I get a rush from my addictive behavior.

There's just something exhilarating about public productivity. It makes me feel strong, worthy. It brings approval and accolades and can keep me going on an adrenaline rush. When I work a fifteen-hour day, I often feel a great sense of accomplishment. I love the high-risk decisions, the writing under pressure, and the raw excitement of ministry. Public productivity can be exhilarating. It stimulates my adrenaline and feeds my ego. (This is why so many people end up with an inflated ego and a deflated family.)

> Don't make the mistake of believing that only "business types" or socialites fall for the empty promises of success, achievement, and public productivity. Achievement addiction can and does affect anybody.

Of course, there's a flip side too. Another reason I keep pushing is that the idea of *not* being publically productive can be downright terrifying. The rewards of achievement are fleeting. The demands are constant. The prospect of failing is always looming . . . and always unthinkable. I never feel I've quite arrived. And so I'm driven to keep pushing, keep trying, keep putting in those long hours at the expense of my relationships, my health, even my soul.

And it's not just me. I see this tendency all the time in people I meet:

- employees who sacrifice relationships to climb the corporate ladder
- entrepreneurs who put all their time and energy into building their dreams
- students who fixate on grades and awards
- parents who throw everything into building the perfect family
- performers who will do anything it takes to be a star
- volunteers who invest long hours in helping others (but crave recognition for it)
- pastors and other church workers who wear themselves out building a public ministry

Don't make the mistake of believing that only "business types" or socialites fall for the empty promises of success, achievement, and public productivity. Achievement addiction can and does affect anybody. And I think we all know that an addiction to public productivity will eventually destroy us. We were never created to find our worth simply in what we do.

HUNGRY FOR MORE

It has practically become a cliché, but it's no less true: God created "human beings," not "human doings." And yet the desire to "do"— to create, climb, contribute, dream, and risk—is a God-given part of what it means to be a human being. Erwin McManus put it this way:

"The reason we struggle with insignificance, the reason we fight to accomplish something, the reason we aspire and dream and risk is that God creates us with an intrinsic need to become."[2]

We were indeed made to do something great with our lives. But for many of us, if not all of us, there is something else going on deep in our hearts that goes well beyond the desire just to do well or to make a difference. Each one of us has been corrupted by what the Bible calls sin, so we start looking to success and accomplishment to give us something only God can give us. Our God-given yearning to become turns into

- I don't just want to have a job. I want to have the best job.
- I don't just want a title. I want a title that sets me apart and allows me to lord it over others.
- I don't just want to raise kids. I want to have beautiful, accomplished kids who make me feel great and make yours look inferior.
- I don't just want to contribute. I want to contribute more than you, and I want everyone to know I contributed more than you. But I don't want to be so blatant about letting everyone know, so I'll find subtle ways that seem humble so I look even better!
- I don't just want to win. I want to win no matter what. In fact, I've got to win in order to feel okay about my life.

That's when the addiction kicks in. And so we lie, we cheat, we backstab, and we manipulate. We gossip, we overwork, we over-stress, we overmedicate—all for our fix of public productivity.

Why? Because success and achievement have become counterfeit gods. And when we bow down to the god of success, we inevitably find ourselves on the constant treadmill of proving ourselves again and again and again.

NOTHING GAINED

The wisest man who ever lived, Solomon, gave us tremendous insight into the frustration that comes along with looking for achievement to give you what only God can give you. He wrote,

> I undertook great projects: I built houses for myself and planted vineyards. I made gardens and parks and planted all kinds of fruit trees in them. I made reservoirs to water groves of flourishing trees. I bought male and female slaves and had other slaves who were born in my house. I also owned more herds and flocks than anyone in Jerusalem before me. I amassed silver and gold for myself, and the treasure of kings and provinces. I acquired male and female singers, and a harem as well—the delights of a man's heart. I became greater by far than anyone in Jerusalem before me. In all this my wisdom stayed with me. (Eccl. 2:4–9)

Now that's one heck of a résumé. Clearly Solomon accomplished it all. He experienced more success than anyone before him. But none of his accomplishments brought him the satisfaction he desired:

> *I denied myself nothing my eyes desired;*
> *I refused my heart no pleasure.*
> *My heart took delight in all my labor,*
> *and this was the reward for all my toil.*
> *Yet when I surveyed all that my hands had done*
> *and what I had toiled to achieve,*
> *everything was meaningless, a chasing after the wind;*
> *nothing was gained under the sun. (vv. 10–11)*

Does any of this sound familiar? Solomon had accumulated money, power, and accomplishments—the biblical version of the larger office, the bigger paycheck, the grander title, the public award. He reached the absolute pinnacle of success, what so many of us have desired for as long as we can remember. But then he discovered it was all meaningless. All pointless. His achievements couldn't satisfy his deep-down cravings for more.

Solomon is not the only one to discover this truth. Pop singer Madonna described the seduction of success like this:

> I have an iron will, and all my will has always been to conquer some horrible feeling of inadequacy. . . . I push past one spell of it and discover myself as a special human being and then I get to another stage and think I'm mediocre and uninteresting. . . . My drive in life is from this horrible fear of being mediocre. And that's always pushing me, pushing me. Because even though I've become Somebody, I still have to prove that I'm *Somebody*. My struggle has never ended and it probably never will.[3]

That's how you feel when get caught up in achievement addiction. You have to prove yourself again and again and again.

In Solomon's case it seems he was running from God instead of to God. He tried to find meaning in absolutely everything except for in God, and his striving left him empty. He was wrapped up in what I call success-based identity.

Success-based identity is the assumption that what you do determines who you are. You try to control the opinions and approval of others through your performance, and you let what they think of you affect what *you* think of you. In other words, you tend to gather your self-worth externally.

And gathering your self-worth externally is kind of like trying to fill up a lake with a Dixie cup. It's just never enough. That's why it's so addictive.

And gathering your self-worth externally is kind of like trying to fill up a lake with a Dixie cup. It's just never enough. That's why it's so addictive.

Now you may already be convinced beyond a doubt that this is an idol you struggle with. But you might be on the fence, so let's dig a little deeper. How do you know if you struggle with idolatry in the area of success and achievement? I want to walk you through a few characteristics of people who deal with this.

TRAP #1: WANTING TO ACHIEVE REGARDLESS OF WHAT IT DOES TO THE PEOPLE AROUND YOU

Often people who have allowed success and achievement to become an idol see to it that they get their way and end up on top as a means of boosting their own sense of worth. Unfortunately, they will do this at the expense of the worth of others.

Achievement addicts can be ruthless or merely insensitive with work colleagues, subordinates, or clients, sometimes with the flimsy excuse of "It's just business" or "It's nothing personal." They'll claim credit for projects, blame others for failures, maneuver themselves into the spotlight, perhaps even fudge the truth.

But the real human sacrifices of achievement addiction are personal relationships, because achievement addicts are no different than any other kind of addict. They'll put a marriage on the sidelines for one more hit. They'll ignore their friends for one more buzz. They'll abandon their kids emotionally for one more night chasing the high or rope their loved ones into serving as support staff for their get-ahead projects.

To make things worse, chances are they'll fool themselves about what they're doing. It's not at all uncommon for an achievement addict to claim—and actually believe—that "I'm doing it all for you."

Could this be an issue in your own life? It might help to consider:

- Are long hours or other work issues a consistent cause of conflict in your marriage or other relationships?
- Do you cancel dinner, church, or a personal gathering at least once a month because you "have to work"?
- Do you ever find yourself excusing your behavior as "It's just business" or "It's nothing personal" or "I'm not doing this for *me*"?

TRAP #2: DEPENDING ON THE APPROVAL OF OTHERS

Several months ago I finished a project I had been working on for almost a year. It was a huge accomplishment, and I genuinely should have felt good about its completion. However, I just sat there at my desk thinking how anticlimactic it felt. Why? Because for the most part, my accomplishment had flown under the radar of others. It hadn't gotten a lot of attention or applause. And that fact left me feeling empty.

It reminded me that for those of us who wrestle with gathering our self-worth externally, it's not really the accomplishment we're after. The *recognition* of the accomplishment is the addictive drug for us.

I'll be talking more about approval addiction in a coming chapter. But for now, here are a few questions to ask yourself:

- Do you often have a need to be noticed or approved of by others to feel good about yourself?
- Do you find yourself bragging to others about how many hours you've been working?
- Do you find yourself stressing out in public over how your kids act because you want others to think you're a good parent?

TRAP #3: CONFUSING WHO YOU ARE
WITH WHAT YOU ACCOMPLISH

One Sunday morning while I was hanging out in the lobby of Cross Point Church, where I pastor, a guy walked up to me and handed me his business card. It's not uncommon for people to approach me and hand me notes or business cards introducing themselves as they walk out of church, so I really didn't think anything about it. I do remember looking down at the card and seeing the logo of a local university before I slipped it into my pocket.

Later that evening while I was emptying out all my pockets (two ibuprofen, three pieces of gum, fourteen cents, several notes), I came upon that business card again. The name on the card was Jon Hanson. Apparently he was some sort of university administrator. Nothing out of the ordinary. But then I flipped the card over and saw an alarming message, written in all caps: "PLEASE CALL ME I NEED HELP."

It was too late to do anything about it that night, so I just lay there in bed wondering what kind of help this guy might need. What was he going through that warranted his getting my attention this way?

I found out when I called the next morning. He was losing his job. The university he worked for was going to announce that very day that they were letting him go.

I remember communicating how sorry I was that he was going through this and assuring him I would be praying for his next steps in finding a new job. He came back with, "No, pastor, I don't think you understand. I don't want another job. In fact, I don't want to live." Something in his voice made me think he wasn't just being dramatic. He was serious.

"I've put my whole life into this job," he continued. "It's every-thing to me. I've put off developing friendships and dating so I could give my best to the job. My entire life revolves around it. And I'm really good at what I do. How could they do this to me?"

Do you see what was happening with Jon? This was certainly a life event worthy of grieving, but he was grieving more than a life event. In his mind he wasn't just losing a job. He was losing himself. He'd made a mistake that so many of us make in our culture today. He had confused who he was with what he did.

Do you wrestle with this? Are you sure? Here are a couple of questions to get you thinking:

- Do you believe that if you make mistakes, you are a failure?
- When you're criticized for your job performance, do you tend to take it personally?
- If you lost your job tomorrow, would you lose your identity?

TRAP #4: ALWAYS NEEDING TO CLIMB ONE RUNG HIGHER

I had a pastor friend admit to me the other day that no matter what attendance records they hit at his church, the numbers were never enough for him. His deepest passion wasn't bringing people to Christ. His passion was to be recognized for hitting a goal—and then beating it.

Mary Bell, a counselor who works with high-level executives in Houston, has seen this phenomenon—and its destructive fallout—again and again.

Achievement, Bell [says] is the alcohol of our time. These days, the best people don't abuse alcohol, they abuse their lives. . . . "You're successful, so good things happen," Bell says. "You complete a project, and you feel dynamite. That feeling doesn't last forever, and you

slide back to normal. You think, 'I've got to start a new project'—
which is still normal. But you love the feeling of euphoria, so you've
got to have it again. The problem is, you can't stay on that high."[4]

So let's say you're working on a big sale at work and it doesn't happen. Your self-esteem is on the line because you've been gathering
your self-worth externally. You're crushed by the failure, but you go
back and try even harder next time. This time you achieve the goal,
but if you're honest, the highs don't seem quite so high. You may make
a sale that's even bigger than the one that got away, but it doesn't give
you that same grand feeling. So you try harder . . . and harder.

Is this a problem for you? Try asking yourself these questions:

- Do you find yourself perpetually dissatisfied regardless of
  what you accomplish at home or work?
- Do you find it difficult to celebrate accomplishments
  because you've already moved on to the next task, job, or
  mission?
- Does completing a project or a goal tend to leave you
  feeling down or even depressed?

TRAP #5: YOU COMPARE YOURSELF WITH OTHERS AND STRUGGLE WHEN OTHERS SUCCEED

People who are looking to success to give them something only God
can give them tend to compare themselves with others or easily fall
into jealousy or resentment. If you struggle with this, you'll often say
(or think) things like:

- "Why didn't *I* get to have lunch with the boss?"
- "Why did *she* get that assignment?"
- "Why did *their kids* get accepted into that school?"

- "Why does *he* get to go to that conference and I don't?"
- "Why did *she* get that raise? I work harder than she does."

From there, it's an easy step to thoughts like these:

- "If she's elected, I need to run for a higher office."
- "If he gets the assignment, I've got to volunteer for a more prestigious project."
- "If the neighbors went to Florida on vacation, we've got to scrape up the money to go to Europe."
- "If Brandon's friend has an inflatable at his birthday party, Brandon's party needs a bigger inflatable . . . and maybe a pony."

You see, if your whole life revolves around getting to the top rung of the ladder and being the best—the most popular musician, the top sales rep, the best parent—you probably don't respond well to feeling average and looking up at others who seem to have climbed higher than you. You might even fall into cynicism and bitterness and look for people to blame for your perceived failures.

A few weeks ago, after an evening out with the guys (which included eating some of the hottest wings I've ever consumed and playing a new card game I'm addicted to, "Dutch Blitz"), I brought up a situation with another pastor. He was someone most of the guys in the group knew, so I felt comfortable enough to spend the next five minutes totally bashing him, poking fun at him, and making light of a situation he was going through. It didn't take long before my friends jumped in

> What we're chasing just doesn't have the ability to give us what we really need. And our efforts at chasing it may cause us to sacrifice what is most important.

on the slam fest. I confess I felt a certain amount of enjoyment hearing them echo my bashing. That was the most enjoyable part of the evening for me, since I ended up getting crushed at the game of cards.

Later, after everyone left, I lay in bed thinking, *Why did I say all those things? Why did I feel such a rush of enjoyment pointing out and then making fun of somebody else's mistakes?* I felt awful. But I also understood why I'd said the things I said. For a short time, gossiping and laughing about somebody else's shortcoming had caused me to feel better about my own.

Why do we do that? Why do we compare? Why does reveling in somebody else's flaws make us feel good about our own situations?

At some level I was jealous of the success or influence the other pastor had. Tearing down someone else's accomplishments was a way to make my own accomplishments look that much grander. Criticism of others is just a cowardly form of self-praise I use to momentarily inflate my sense of self-worth.

Do you struggle with this? Here are a few questions to ask:

- Do you regularly use humor to put others down just for a laugh?
- Do you find yourself criticizing others in order to feel better about yourself?
- Do you often compare yourself to other people?
- Do you tend to covet another's accomplishments more than celebrate them?
- When a colleague or partner is praised or rewarded, do you usually feel glad . . . or grumpy?

THE BIGGEST LOSERS

I had several subsequent conversations with my new friend Jon, who had lost his job. As weeks passed, although the pain of the dismissal continued, he started to realize just how dependent he had been on his career to bring him a sense of satisfaction. He had started to believe something like this: *If I'm seen as successful in my work, then I won't feel inadequate. I won't have fear. I won't have self-doubt. I'll be somebody.*

That's the inner logic behind all achievement addiction. The details may vary, but the underlying assumption is the same—that we *need* success in order to be satisfied and to feel worthwhile. Yet all we accrue as we climb that achievement ladder is more pressure and fear and anxiety and even self-doubt.

What we're chasing just doesn't have the ability to give us what we really need. And our efforts at chasing it may cause us to sacrifice what is most important.

Jesus honed in on the reality when he asked, "What good will it be for someone to gain the whole world, yet forfeit their soul? Or what can anyone give in exchange for their soul?" (Matt. 16:26).

Jesus knew that success and achievement are just a few of the many shiny things that try to grab our eyes here on this earth. They look valuable. They look fulfilling. They claim they can meet the desires of our hearts, but they cannot. Not even close. They are nothing but empty promises. The big lie that could cost us everything.

Jesus is saying that the people who lose their souls, even to gain the greatest success and achievement, make a horrible deal. Those who become caught in an achievement addiction can walk away as unspeakable losers.

POSITION-BASED IDENTITY

So what's the alternative? How can we break free from an addiction to public productivity? How can we answer that inner call for meaning and purpose without becoming overly dependent on success and achievement? How can we obey our God-given drive to make a difference without falling for the empty promises of more, more, more?

As I've said, this is an ongoing issue in my own life. But my goal these days—a goal I proposed to Jon as well and that I'm proposing to you—is to transition from a success-based identity to a position-based identity.

What is a position-based identity? It means that instead of gathering self-worth externally—from achievement—we try to receive it internally. We begin to understand that self-worth comes from who we are in Christ, not what we accomplish in this world.

Does this mean we don't work hard, that we don't care about results? Does it mean we don't strive to be a great stay-at-home mom or win the next football game or write the next hit song?

No, not at all. It just means our identity is not totally wrapped up in what we accomplish.

A few months ago I stepped aboard the plushest, most luxurious tour bus I had ever seen. Seriously, if someone would have told me that a bus could be that nice, I would have bought one years ago. Who needs a house when you can have that?

On the bus I had a talk with one of the most successful people in the music industry. This young woman has won almost every award there is to win and has shattered numerous records in her field. She is an unqualified success. But she also gets her fair share of criticism. At times it's thoughtless, unwarranted, and extremely vulgar. Despite her accomplishments, the criticism has taken a toll on this young woman's spirit.

After listening to her story and realizing she is actually handling the situation quite well under the circumstances, I offered her this thought: "You understand you're more than your giftedness, right? You're more than a great voice. You're more than a chart-topping act. You're more than a ticket someone purchases. You're a living, breathing human being God thought into existence. You matter to him."

While heading back to the hotel room that night, I prayed that those words would choke out the many voices bombarding this young performer and penetrate her heart. And I pray they will sink into your heart in this moment.

You, too, are more than your giftedness.

You're more than the title on your office door or the company on your business card.

You're more than what your home looks like or how your kids act.

You're more than what you accomplished last week or last month—more than anything you could accomplish in your lifetime.

Once you embrace this truth, you can begin to deal more objectively in any circumstance because your sense of worth and identity isn't up for grabs.

Positional-based identity doesn't come from your performance or from anyone else's evaluation of your performance. Rather, positional-based identity comes from how you feel about your position in Christ.

Psalm 139 says that we are "fearfully and wonderfully made" (v. 14). Just the fact that you're here, that you exist, that God made you who you are, means that you're somebody. You matter. You are loved, treasured, valued. And your value is not up for grabs—no matter how successful or unsuccessful you are.

What if you set this book down for a moment and just asked God,

- "Did you really make me?"
- "Did you put me together before I breathed a breath?"
- "Did you know before I was born that I'd be reading this book and talking to you right now?"
- "Am I really important to you, just as I am?"

What if you moved beyond the cognizant understanding that God made you and loves you and focused instead on what that means?

You are not your giftedness. God didn't make a singer. God didn't make an accountant. God didn't make a preacher. You are not any more valuable or less valuable to God because of your job title, your tax bracket, or your social status. Even if you lose your job, even if you're struggling in your family, even if you make a mistake, God's affection for you does not waver. Your value in his eyes does not decline.

> You are not your giftedness. God didn't make a singer. God didn't make an accountant. God didn't make a preacher. You are not any more valuable or less valuable to God because of your job title, your tax bracket, or your social status.

Yes, you are made to do great things, and it's wonderful to work hard. It's a blessing to use your gifts and talents. But your worth, your value, is not based on your achievements. Letting anything other than Christ define you will grind you down. You will always be on a treadmill of achievement, always be haunted by the thought that you're not doing enough, always be hungry for the "fix" of public productivity.

Scripture teaches that you are to root your identity not in what *you* have accomplished, but what has been accomplished *for* you. John 1:12 states this succinctly: "To all who did receive him, to those who believed in his name, he gave the right to become children of God."

Is the root of your identity in the truth that *right now* you are loved?

Do you believe that right now you are accepted, that right now you are enough because you are the beloved child of the King?

Basing your identity on that reality is the only way to treat an achievement addiction. It's the only way to tear down the ladder and destroy the treadmill of achievement and success. Because if you do that, your life will be rooted in something that cannot be shaken.

And then you'll be free to really make a difference.

CHAPTER FOUR
ADDICTED TO APPROVAL

Eighteen-month-old Sean realized every person's greatest fear when his mother left their apartment with no intention of ever coming back. He and his siblings were discovered days later, abandoned, alone, and hungry, when a neighbor realized something was amiss and called the fire department.

That day in St. Louis, Missouri, Sean was launched on a long and draining journey that would include nine or ten foster homes before he was finally adopted at age four. At last somebody wanted him. At last somebody thought he was worth loving. To a foster child, adoption is a big stamp of approval.

Except, in Sean's case, it wasn't.

The man and woman who adopted Sean would eventually have four of their own children and two adopted kids. But Sean stood out. He told me, "I was a high-energy kid. I went to bed late at night and got up early in the morning. I was constantly excited and rambunctious, and it was just too much for my adoptive parents to handle. They had no idea how to deal with me. They always wanted me to be more like their first son, my older brother, who was quiet, well behaved, and extremely athletic.

"I imagined they wanted to give me back. Instead, they decided early on that they would break me like a horse."

For the next ten to twelve years, Sean's life was hell. He couldn't do anything right. His father, especially, couldn't control his anger toward him and was physically and mentally abusive. The continual rejection was too much for Sean, and he turned to food to ease his pain. He remembers, "I would sneak food into my closet at night. I ate and ate and ate trying to numb the pain. When my stomach was full I felt satisfied, even if it was for only moments."

By his junior year of high school, Sean weighed over 320 pounds.

In college Sean discovered a relationship with God and began to understand what true acceptance and love was all about, but he still hadn't dealt with his childhood wounds. He got married at twenty-six, and by twenty-eight, still eating food to try to numb the pain of not being accepted, he weighed almost 470 pounds.

THE EMOTIONAL ROLLER COASTER

Over the years I've spent hundreds of hours counseling individuals who are in an absolute tailspin emotionally because someone doesn't

- approve of them;
- accept them;
- affirm them;
- want them;
- care for them;
- appreciate them;
- love them.

I'm not just talking about deprived or abused foster kids like Sean. Some of the most dysfunctional adults I know grew up in homes where they were given almost everything—toys, attention, opportunities. What they *didn't* get was a sense that they were valued, treasured, cared for.

They don't always turn to food like my friend Sean. Some comfort themselves with alcohol or pills. Some cycle through relationships. Some, as I've indicated, fall for the empty promises of success and achievement. I've seen people get stuck in some pretty devastating and destructive behavior patterns, all to find that elusive approval of another human being.

There are few things people fear as much as we fear being unwanted, rejected, and alone. It's so easy to fall into thinking,

- *If I had her love . . .*
- *If I had my boss's acceptance . . .*
- *If my dad just valued me . . .*
- *. . . it would fix my life.*

It's so easy to fall into the trap of expecting relationships to give our lives meaning.

Not that there's anything wrong with wanting relationships. Just as we've been designed to seek out meaning and purpose, we're also designed to yearn for emotional and physical closeness. Our connections with friends, family, colleagues, and community are crucial to navigating life successfully. Our desire to know and be known and accepted for who we are is not a perversion or sinful desire.

But there's another side to this. I'm a huge fan of community. I believe in relationships. I quite often write and preach about how important and essential our connections with other people are. But today I want to remind you of what community cannot do for us. As Henri Nouwen wrote,

We constantly feel tempted to want more from those around us than they can give. We relate to our neighbors with the hope and the supposition that they are able to fulfill most of our deepest needs, and then we find ourselves disillusioned, angry, and frustrated when they do not.[1]

I believe most of us understand this—intellectually, at least. We know that when we expect someone else to

- complete us,
- take our pain away,
- understand us completely,
- heal us,
- make us feel good about ourselves,
- always be with us,

we are expecting something that another human being cannot give.

But our loneliness and brokenness may still push us to expect it anyway—it happens all the time. We may even fall into the trap of attaching all our God-given longings for meaning and affirmation to a single person or group.

That's the trap of approval addiction.

The drug addict needs the fix. The alcoholic needs the buzz.

And approval addicts depend exclusively on other people to love them, care for them, affirm them, and give them meaning.

Our culture has many names for this kind of emotional neediness, and it manifests in many different ways. Sometimes it's called co-dependency or love addiction. It can be focused on one person ("I need you in my life") or directed toward other people in general ("I'm a people pleaser"). It can also piggyback onto other dysfunctions, such as substance abuse, sexual addiction, or destructive family problems.

Whatever it's called and however it manifests, approval addiction is the process of looking to people or relationships to provide the love, acceptance, and validation that should come from God.

And that, of course, is idolatry.

Such idolatry generates inaccurate readings about life. It distorts our feeling and thinking by spitting out false definitions of success and failure and love and worth. And it can simply wear us out—because life as an approval addict is difficult and exhausting.

We find ourselves constantly checking to make sure we've said the right thing, done the right thing, and looked the right way in order to get the affirmation we crave. Our feelings are held captive on an out-of-control emotional roller coaster. We go from feeling the wonderful highs that come from getting an approval "fix" to the deep despair that comes when our "supply," the human source of our love and approval, shuts down, gets angry or judgmental, or goes away altogether.

And when that inevitably happens—when the person or relationship we're depending on fails us—we may start thinking things like

- *I can't do anything right.*
- *Nobody will ever care about me.*
- *Something's wrong with me.*
- *I'm not worth loving.*
- *I can never be forgiven.*
- *There's no point in even trying.*

Such thinking can make us needy and demanding or emotionally frozen, absolutely paralyzed by the fear of rejection. Self-esteem
becomes so fragile that even the lightest constructive criticism can
destroy us emotionally. We're so desperate to be loved and supported
that we have no resources to love and affirm anyone else. So ironically, this distorted sense of reality can actually destroy or distort the
very relationships we depend on.

LOOKING FOR LOVE

The story of Jacob, which begins in Genesis 25, has to be one of the
strangest stories in the entire Bible. Stories like this are one of the reasons I know God's Word is true. If someone was making this stuff up,
there's no way they would have included stories like this in the Bible.

Jacob was the son of Isaac and Rebekah. His twin brother, Esau,
had been born minutes before, making him the younger of the two.
For reasons beyond my understanding, Isaac noticeably favored
Esau, and this favoritism created a huge wound in Jacob's life. In
response to this rejection, Jacob formed an unhealthy attachment to
his mother, Rebekah.

Since Esau was the oldest brother, he stood to receive a great
inheritance from his father as well as something equally coveted—a
special blessing. But one day Jacob and his mother conspired to trick
the aging Isaac into giving the blessing to Jacob. And their plan actually
worked. Isaac inadvertently gave Jacob the blessing. Esau was furious
when he found out. He vowed to kill his brother, so Jacob ran away.

And you thought your family was messed up?

At this point Jacob's life was in ruins. He was running for his
life, sure he would never see his family again. His twin brother hated
him. And he had lost his ill-gotten inheritance because he had to run
away. In a desperate state, Jacob traveled to live with his mother's
family—specifically, her brother Laban.

Are you still with me? Let's pick up this story as told in Genesis 29.

> Now Laban had two daughters; the name of the older was Leah, and the name of the younger was Rachel. Leah had weak eyes, but Rachel had a lovely figure and was beautiful. Jacob was in love with Rachel and said, "I'll work for you seven years in return for your younger daughter Rachel."
>
> Laban said, "It's better that I give her to you than to some other man. Stay here with me." So Jacob served seven years to get Rachel, but they seemed like only a few days to him because of his love for her. (vv. 16–20)

So when Jacob arrived at his uncle Laban's place, he learned that Laban had two daughters. According to Scripture, not me, Leah was the older, less attractive one. Rachel, on the other hand, had "a lovely figure and was beautiful." In other words, Rachel was "hot." And Jacob fell for her hard. He agreed to work seven years for his uncle in order to marry her.

Now, scholars point out that this was an unheard-of price to pay for a bride. It was at least four times the normal price. But Jacob was so smitten with Rachel that he was willing to pay what Laban asked. He worked the full seven years and then said to Laban, "Give me my wife. My time is completed, and I want to make love to her" (v. 21). Even after seven years, he was overwhelmed with emotional and sexual longing for that woman.

Sounds kind of romantic—a man willing to wait and work for the woman he loved? In our culture this type of story is celebrated, maybe even longed for. We would make a movie out of it—although these days we would turn all the characters into really pale, sparkly vampires.

But do you understand why Jacob was acting like this? If you think about it, he was showing all the signs of approval addiction.

His life was empty. He had never had his father's love. He was separated from his mother, with whom he had a very close relationship. His own actions had created a rift with his only brother. And because of the circumstances, he had no real sense of God's love for him. He was essentially alone and felt abandoned. His one hope was Rachel, and he pinned all his needs and yearnings on her.

If I had Rachel's love, he probably thought, *it would give me meaning. If I had her acceptance, I would feel like somebody again.* He was depending on the love and acceptance of one person to give him what only God could give him. And as we've seen, no human being is capable of that.

If you're familiar with this story, you know what happened next. Laban tricked Jacob into marrying the wrong girl. Jacob woke up the morning after the wedding and realized he was lying in bed next to Leah—the older, less attractive sister. Tim Keller summarized the deep poignancy of this passage:

> We learn that through all of life there runs a ground note of cosmic disappointment. . . . Jacob said, "If I can just get Rachel, everything will be okay." And he goes to bed with the one who he thinks is Rachel, and literally, the Hebrew says, "in the morning, behold, it was Leah" (Genesis 29:25). One commentator noted about this verse, "This is a miniature of our disillusionment, experienced from Eden onwards." What does that mean? With all respect to this woman . . . it means that no matter what we put our hopes in, in the morning, *it is always Leah, never Rachel.*[2]

Not surprisingly Jacob was angry, disappointed, and hurt. He had been tricked by his uncle. He had married a girl he did not love. He had worked seven years for a woman he desired deeply and he still didn't have.

But look at what Jacob did next. He agreed to work an *additional* seven years for Laban so he could also marry Rachel.

I believe Jacob was doing exactly what you and I have done over and over throughout our lives. He was using the love and acceptance of another human being—or the promise of such love and acceptance—to medicate his pain and fuel his insanity. He would eventually marry Rachel, but his unhealthy dependence on her would cause decades of misery and disaster in his family line.

THE FALLOUT

Are you like Jacob? Do you struggle with the tendency to depend on another person to make you feel loved, wanted, accepted, and approved of? Will you take the time to honestly evaluate your own life?

- Do you constantly worry about what others might be thinking of you?
- Do you refrain from doing a lot of things because other people may not approve?
- Do you tend to replay criticisms over and over in your head?
- Do you feel that having a significant other in your life is crucial to your happiness—that you are somehow "less than" if you're not in a serious relationship?
- Do you get really anxious when you think an important person in your life might be upset with you?

I'm quite convinced after years of casual observation that the majority of the population suffers from varying degrees of approval addiction, and some are entirely unaware of it. This is an excruciating condition because there will always be someone who doesn't like, love, or approve of some part of us.

Now, you can live and survive and still make a life chasing after this empty promise, but there are a few things I can almost guarantee will happen. People who live their lives hoping that someone else's love and approval will meet their deepest desires will be destined for three things.

DESTINED FOR MEDIOCRITY

Approval addicts are destined for a life of mediocrity because they always have to follow the herd—and that's the very opposite of what Christ calls us to. He insists that we follow *him* instead, and sometimes that means taking risks, making unpopular stands, going against the flow, even upsetting people. How can you do that when you're depending on other people for validation? When an approval addict attempts to break out and take a risk, what typically happens is that the herd criticizes or even attacks, pushing hard until the errant one falls back with the rest of the crowd.

> If you depend on other people approving or supporting everything you say or do, you will end up doing and saying nothing. You will be handcuffed to mediocrity.

When I was in college, I felt God calling me to start a church. I was twenty-one and the youth pastor at a small rural church. I decided to resign from that position to follow what I felt God was prompting me to do with my life. But one night after I had given notice but was still finishing out my commitment to the first church, I overheard two deacons talking. I had been working late and just happened to walk past the church library on my way out the door. I heard my name, so I decided to stop and listen. (I could be wrong, but I don't think it counts as eavesdropping if you hear your name mentioned.)

The two men were talking about my resignation and my desire to start a church. Clearly, they thought the whole thing was a huge joke. "Does this kid think he can actually be a pastor? Does he think he can preach? Who in the world is going to follow a twenty-one-year-old leader?"

It's not like I hadn't thought about all those questions myself. But to hear them from a couple of men I'd looked up to was crushing. I fought tears as I walked out to my car. I got in and I prayed, "God, those guys are right. Who do I think I am? I can't do this. They know it. I know it. Everyone knows it."

That night, though, I felt God reassure me that I was not living for the approval of other people. My goal in life was not to seek everyone's permission and approval but to live the life I felt God was calling me to live.

Starting that church changed the entire trajectory of my life and my faith in God. I'm even grateful to those two guys in the church library because they taught me something important: If you depend on other people approving or supporting everything you say or do, you will end up doing and saying nothing. You will be handcuffed to mediocrity.

DESTINED FOR EXHAUSTION

Few things will wear you down like trying to control your image in the eyes of other people. I don't know about you, but I have definitely found myself in this trap, caring too much about what people think of me. I spend so much energy projecting and predicting and wondering what impression I'm making that I lose track of the really important question: Am I doing what God has called and designed me to do?

Several years ago I found myself in an uncomfortable position at the church I now pastor in Nashville. The church was growing fast, and my responsibilities as pastor were shifting. I could no longer personally minister to all the people who called Cross Point home. But I stubbornly kept trying to do all the counseling, all the weddings, all the messages, and all the meetings. This schedule left me so depleted that I had very little time or energy left for my family and friends.

At the time, I thought my attempts to be all things to all people came from a desire to be loving. I now look back and realize that my primary motivation was not to be loving but to be loved. And there is a huge difference between the two, isn't there?

I discovered that if I really wanted to be loving, I needed to allow the other pastors on our staff to step up and minister. That was a difficult transition for me since for years I had derived so much of my validation through the pats on the back I received from church members. But I've gradually learned to treasure what happens when I let myself step back and depend on God for my validation. More people are served. More people know the joy of using their gifts in ministry. My important relationships—with my wife, my children, my close friends, and my God—have room to grow. I feel energized instead of feeling exhausted and depleted. And because I'm tapping into the Source of dependable love, I feel more valued and confident.

DESTINED FOR DISAPPOINTMENT AND REJECTION

Approval addiction is essentially an act of self-abandonment. Instead of finding your value and worth from your Creator, you have essentially given your heart up for adoption. You have given it away to others for love and approval, making them responsible for your feelings.

The trouble is, no human being on earth is up to that responsibility. Every single human you will ever encounter is a sinner. Everyone has the potential to disappoint you, betray you, and reject you—usually because of his or her own neediness. And even those who love you well and don't let you down (much) will eventually die and leave you. Depending on anyone other than God for fundamental validation is just asking for heartbreak.

But the idea of depending on God may be problematic for you. You might be saying, "Are you kidding me? I can't find acceptance from the people around me, even from people like my parents, who are obligated to accept me but don't. You think I can find acceptance from God? You clearly don't know a lot about my life."

That may be true. But I also think your painful relationship experiences might be pushing you away from what you need most. The same is true with your feelings of guilt over what you've done and your shame over what has been done to you. Some people live with so much of this that, in a very ironic twist, they hide from the one Person who can give what they so desperately need.

This reminds me so much of Adam and Eve in the garden. When they sinned, what was their reaction? Their first instinct was to run away and hide from God. I'm amazed to this day how strong my temptation is to hide my sin and pain from God and others.

We act as if God is shocked to discover we make mistakes, that our lives are less than perfect. He is not in heaven wringing his hands and saying, "Oh no! When I created you, I had no idea you would act like this." You are no surprise to him. He knows you through and through, as Psalm 139 reminds us:

> *You know when I sit and when I rise;*
> *you perceive my thoughts from afar.*
> *You discern my going out and my lying down;*
> *you are familiar with all my ways.*
> *Before a word is on my tongue*
> *you, LORD, know it completely. (vv. 2–4)*

Do you see what this means? Even with all his foreknowledge of our weaknesses and the mistakes we will make, God still chose us on purpose and brought us into relationship with him. He has no problem with our shortcomings; he's completely equipped to handle them. We're the ones who have a problem with our failures. We're the ones who keep on suffering from our guilt and shame instead of accepting God's love and his help for handling our sin. We're the ones who would rather hide than admit to ourselves or anyone else that we are less than perfect.

> Approval addiction is essentially an act of self-abandonment. Instead of finding your value and worth from your Creator, you have essentially given your heart up for adoption. You have given it away to others for love and approval, making them responsible for your feelings.

You may have made horrible mistakes and need to know God still loves you. You may have been cruelly sinned against and need the reassurance that God would never treat you that way. No matter what has happened or what will happen, God's response to you is the same. You are his. You are loved. You are accepted. You will never, ever lose your value in God's eyes.

Sometimes the most absurd things we do are in response to our lack of confidence in our true identity. Not knowing who we are or were even meant to become, we foolishly try to become something we are not. But Scripture assures us that our exalted position in Christ is not a hypothetical thing or a goal for which we strive. It is an accomplished fact:

> Since, then, you have been raised with Christ, set your hearts on things above, where Christ is, seated at the right hand of God. Set your minds on things above, not on earthly things. For you died, and your life is now hidden with Christ in God. When Christ, who is your life, appears, then you also will appear with him in glory. (Col. 3:1–4)

Do you understand the implications of that? Your worth and value aren't determined by anyone's love and acceptance except for God's. And God's love and acceptance is already guaranteed. If you look to him for love and approval, you will never be rejected.

RELIEF

"Pastor Pete, I've slept with dozens of guys at my high school." That was not exactly what I was expecting to come out of the mouth of the cute, innocent-looking sixteen-year-old girl sitting in my office.

I don't do a lot of counseling with teenagers, but Caroline's mom is a longtime friend of mine, and I could tell she was desperate when she called me. "Pete, I don't know what's happening to my daughter. She's depressed all the time, and I think she's been dabbling in drugs. Ever since Stephen and I divorced, she's been in this emotional spiral. She's known you since she was a little girl. I think she'll listen to you. Will you please talk to her?"

Caroline's heart-stopping confession came right after she had described the pain and emptiness she had felt since her father left her mom almost two years prior. It wasn't hard to see what she was doing. Getting the attention and the "love" of the boys in her school was her way of filling the void left by her absent father. It was her way of feeling desired and affirmed as a woman. But of course, giving herself away over and over had just produced more feelings of being unwanted. No wonder she had turned to drugs. She was trying to escape the pain and disappointment that relationships had created in her life.

The trouble is, no human being on earth is up to that responsibility.

That day in my office, I decided to read Caroline the story about Jesus and the woman at the well. Whether we realize it or not, I think a great number of us can identify with the woman's search for the elusive love of another person.

Now he had to go through Samaria. So he came to a town in Samaria called Sychar, near the plot of ground Jacob had given to his son Joseph. Jacob's well was there, and Jesus, tired as he was from the journey, sat down by the well. It was about noon.

When a Samaritan woman came to draw water, Jesus said to her, "Will you give me a drink?" (His disciples had gone into the town to buy food.) (John 4:4–8)

The time of day is an interesting fact in this story. It's interesting because it was very unusual for someone to go to the well to get water at noon, the hottest part of the day. Most people went for water in the cool of the morning or evening. But we'll see in just a second exactly why this woman was there in the blazing sun.

The Samaritan woman said to him, "You are a Jew and I am a Samaritan woman. How can you ask me for a drink?" (For Jews do not associate with Samaritans.)

Jesus answered her, "If you knew the gift of God and who it is that asks you for a drink, you would have asked him and he would have given you living water."

"Sir," the woman said, "you have nothing to draw with and the well is deep. Where can you get this living water? Are you greater than our father Jacob, who gave us the well and drank from it himself, as did also his sons and his livestock?"

Jesus answered, "Everyone who drinks this water will be thirsty again, but whoever drinks the water I give them will never thirst. Indeed, the water I give them will become in them a spring of water welling up to eternal life."

The woman said to him, "Sir, give me this water so that I won't get thirsty and have to keep coming here to draw water." (vv. 9–15)

He had her attention at this point. She was interested. She was seeking. But look at what Jesus did next. It almost seems a little out of character for him.

> He told her, "Go, call your husband and come back."
> "I have no husband," she replied.
> Jesus said to her, "You are right when you say you have no husband. The fact is, you have had five husbands, and the man you now have is not your husband. What you have just said is quite true." (vv. 16–18)

This was the Samaritan woman's biggest fear—being outed like this. It's why she was there in the middle of the day, when nobody else was around. She was avoiding people. She was ashamed and fearful. She was hiding.

Quite honestly we don't know a lot about this woman. However, we can assume that when she was ten years old, she'd never dreamed her life would end up like this. She'd never imagined she would end up jumping from marriage to marriage to marriage, desperately trying to find this elusive love, acceptance, and approval. She'd never thought she would have to surrender herself to the false and empty acceptance of living and sleeping with a man who wasn't her husband. Her search for love had hurt her again and again and again.

At some point, most likely, the Samaritan woman confused sex and acceptance—a common mistake in our culture today. It's the same mistake Caroline was making. You, too, may have made or are making the mistake of giving yourself away sexually in search of love, hopping from one relationship to another, hoping to be healed and whole.

Let me tell you what I told Caroline that day after reading this story. I said, "Caroline, I know that for me to tell you that sex has been created by God to be enjoyed only inside the confines of marriage makes me sound like I'm way out of touch with culture. I get that. In fact, you might be right. I might be out of touch with culture. But is it possible that you might be out of touch with your soul?

> There is only one way I know how to find relief from crippling approval addiction, and it's found in the unconditional love and acceptance of our heavenly Father.

"You were not created to give yourself away like you do. It's not going to help you heal the wound your father created, and it's certainly not going to help you find the acceptance and approval you so desire."

There is only one way I know how to find relief from crippling approval addiction, and it's found in the unconditional love and acceptance of our heavenly Father. As Erwin McManus wrote,

> You will spend your life working through relationships trying to understand your need for love, your inadequacies in love, your desperation for love, and all the time you might miss the signs that your heart is giving you, that you're searching for God.[3]

Our desire for approval can only truly be met by receiving God's acceptance and approval of us. Unlike human love, God's love will never let us down. This is a consistent message throughout his Word:

- "The LORD himself goes before you and will be with you; he will never leave you nor forsake you" (Deut. 31:8).
- "As a mother comforts her child, so will I comfort you" (Isa. 66:13).
- "Before I formed you in the womb I knew you, before you were born I set you apart" (Jer. 1:5).
- "I have loved you with an everlasting love; I have drawn you with unfailing kindness" (Jer. 31:3).

- "For God so loved the world that he gave his one and only Son, that whoever believes in him shall not perish but have eternal life" (John 3:16).
- "But God demonstrates his own love for us in this: While we were still sinners, Christ died for us" (Rom. 5:8).

This is the love and acceptance we've been longing for, the cure for our approval addiction.

You're likely wondering whatever happened to my friend Sean. Well, this story has an amazing ending. Knowing he could not allow the destructive habits he had formed to mask the pain from his parents' rejection to continue, he decided to do something about it.

It was a long shot, but he tried out to be on the überpopular NBC hit show *The Biggest Loser*. Out of three hundred thousand people who tried out to be on the show, Sean was selected. He lost two hundred pounds on that show. Since his season ended he has lost an additional fifty pounds.

Sean told me, "I made a decision that I was going to stop listening to the whispers of my parents' voices telling me I wasn't good enough and that I would never amount to anything. I was going to stop paying attention to the voices of people who looked down on me or made fun of me because I was different. Instead, I chose to listen to the voice of Christ. He's the only one I'm ultimately living for."

It's amazing the transformation that begins to happen in our lives when we put away the idol of human love, acceptance, and approval. Can you do that? Will you stop listening to those who cannot or will not give you what you need and start listening and leaning into the only One whose approval truly matters?

CHAPTER FIVE
THE PERILS OF POWER

One week not long ago I was working through a very impor-tant church issue with our elders. We have six elders to whom I'm accountable at our church. Our weeklong e-mail correspondence on an issue had resulted in a late-night conference call. About halfway through the two-hour call, I realized I was probably not going to get my way on the issue we were discussing. I had some strong opinions about it, but others had a differing opinion. I remember getting more and more agitated by the minute.

No decision was made that night, but it was clear things wouldn't go the way I wanted it to go. I hung up the phone and felt rage shoot through my body. I was sitting at my desk in my home office, and I slammed my right hand on the desk. Then I took my left arm and literally raked everything on my desk off onto the floor.

I immediately felt stupid for doing that. So I just sat there in silence for the next thirty minutes or so.

Why was I so upset?

Why was I so angry?

As embarrassing as it is to admit, I was on a bit of a power trip. The meeting's outcome was a stark reminder that maybe I didn't have the power and control I thought I did.

Bottom line: I didn't get my way, and I was throwing a tantrum.

Isn't that typical of our outbursts in life? We want to drive fast and get mad at cars blocking the lane. We want a promotion and don't get it and begin hating on the person who did get it. We want to be married and get angry at God because we're still single. And we especially want to beat out everybody else for the prizes in life.

C. S. Lewis once pointed out that

> what we call "ambition" usually means the wish to be more conspicuous or more successful than someone else. It is this competitive element in it that is bad. It is perfectly reasonable to want to dance well or to look nice. But when the dominant wish is to dance better or look nicer than the others—when you begin to feel that if the others danced as well as you or looked as nice as you, that would take all the fun out of it—then you are going wrong.[1]

So true, isn't it? Power at its worst is a sin of comparison.

It's not enough to be a strong leader. We have to be the *strongest* leader.

Power at its worst is a sin of comparison.

It's not enough to have (or be) a pretty wife. We have to have (or be) the *prettiest* wife.

It's not enough to climb the ladder. We have to be at the top of the ladder.

It's not enough to be a good mom. We have to be seen as the best mom.

It's not enough to be a good pastor. We want to be known as the best pastor.

We have to constantly see ourselves as better, more deserving, and more right than everyone else. Which is why so many of us keep falling for the empty promises of power and control.

THE POWER DRUG

I'm not sure there is a more potent, more addictive drug than power. I hate this drug because it has taunted me like a dangling carrot most of my life. I hate it because I've seen more friends run their lives, their marriages, and their careers into a ditch because of its empty promises. To me, it seems more destructive—and seductive—than almost any other single idol.

I read an interesting article recently about a guy named Nick Binkley. Nick was the vice-chairman of Bank of America and a member of its board of directors. Lots of power, to say the least.

But because of a merger situation, Nick decided to resign from his position. The sudden transition from being the vice-chair of one of the largest banks in the world to being without the position turned out to be much harder than he expected. Jeffrey Pfeffer, who related Binkley's story in his book *Power*, explained:

> To be a public figure and perform at a high level requires an intensity that produces, in [Binkley's] words, "a caffeinated high." When you leave such a position and that level of activity ceases, it is almost, as Binkley put it, "Like a car going from ninety miles an hour to a dead stop." When the adrenaline rush ceases, there is a visceral, physiological reaction. In addition to the change in activity and intensity level, there is also the change from being the center of a universe of people fawning over you and heeding your every request to a more "normal" and less-in-the-limelight existence.[2]

Binkley's story may be an extreme case. Most of us don't run in his high-flying circles. But at some level I think most of us can identify

with the addictive pleasure of having power over people and events in
our lives—and the painful frustration that comes with feeling powerless. For instance:

- Do you get very upset when people don't specifically do
  things the way you want them to be done?
- Do you have a hard time following the rules other people
  establish? Do you often believe you know a better way?
- When things go wrong, do you tend to shift blame to others?
- Do you find yourself needing to win every single
  argument you're in?
- Do you sometimes "play games" or manipulate others to
  get your way?
- Do you often lose your temper when situations don't go
  your way?
- Do tool malfunctions (car trouble, computer trouble, etc.)
  really push your buttons?
- Have you ever been told you have "control issues"?

You see, power is not something only CEOs, pastors, politicians,
and business professionals struggle with. Power tempts most if not
all of us.

If winning every argument is an issue with you, it may not be
because you're so passionate about the truth. Could you be craving
the power that comes with dominating another human being?

Or maybe you seek a certain leadership position in the church or
at work or in your neighborhood. Is it really because you want to serve
others, or do you seek the power that comes with lording it over others?

You may have a strong desire to sleep with someone. Are you
really attracted to the person—or to the power of knowing you *could*
sleep with him or her if you wanted to?

I'm not saying that all arguments or leadership campaigns or even sexual relationships involve unhealthy power trips. Not at all. Remember, at the center of every idol we worship is an underlying God-given appetite. The problem comes when we turn to someone or something other than God to fulfill it. That's true of power too.

I'm learning that people don't usually seek power because they desire to become belligerent, self-seeking persons. The initial attraction to power usually begins with a God-given appetite for purpose.

Most of us are wired to want to make a difference.

We want our lives to count for something great.

We want our lives to embody significance.

And somewhere in our journey, we begin to believe that being in control will actually fulfill that desire. That having power and wielding it will somehow make us matter.

That's when our natural yearning for significance becomes something else entirely. That's when we begin worshipping the idol of power—and setting ourselves up for a big fall.

THE BIG FALL

Not long ago I had breakfast with a man named Paul Stanley. Paul looks and sounds like just an average guy, but the past two years for him have been anything but ordinary. Just two short years ago, in fact, Paul was riding a rocket ship to the top of the Tennessee political scene. He was easily one of the most powerful men in our state.

All of this came to a crashing halt when news broke that Paul was having an affair with his twenty-two-year-old intern. To make matters worse, the young woman's boyfriend had attempted to extort ten thousand dollars from Paul in order to keep the story, which included racy photos, under wraps. Paul cooperated with the FBI to bring the boyfriend to justice, but the young man's arrest and conviction catapulted this story into the national headlines.

In one day Paul went from being State Republican Senator Paul

Stanley, chair of the Commerce, Labor and Agriculture Committee, to Paul Stanley, the scum of the earth. Shortly afterward, he resigned his senate seat.

Today Paul Stanley admits that his desire for power played a crucial role in his ultimate demise. "I soaked up the recognition and attention like a sponge," Paul told me. "I was attracted to politics because it got me to the front of the line. I could pick up the phone and get any CEO in the state to talk with me within minutes, and it felt good. It wasn't about me, but it was about my position and the power that came along with it."

When asked when he knew he was going to have an affair with his intern, he answered, "The moment I laid eyes on her. That's what power does. It makes you think you can have anything you want. That you're bigger than the rules."

Paul was experiencing what Tim Keller called "one of the great ironies of sin." Keller wrote, "When human beings try to become more than human beings, to be as gods, they fall to become lower than human beings. To be your own God and live for your own glory and power leads to the most bestial and cruel kind of behavior."[3]

> When a power worshipper smashes his nose against the limits of his control, everyone suffers.

Obviously the truckloads of power Paul Stanley accrued did not keep his house of cards from collapsing. After his scandal broke, he told me, "I went from six hundred miles per hour to zero overnight. When I woke up and I was no longer Senator Paul Stanley, it was like my drink and my line of cocaine were taken away from me. I thrived on the power of the office. I thrived on the attention. I went through a heavy withdrawal period.

"Along with power comes people telling you all the time how great you are because they want something from you. It becomes addictive, and it overinflates your ego and makes you begin to believe 'it's all about me.' I had friendships five miles long and a quarter of an inch deep."

WAKE-UP CALL

The Bible is full of individuals whose worship of power ultimately became their downfalls. Their power and pride became a glaring sun that blinded them from a plethora of deadly traps. One of my favorite examples of this comes from the Old Testament book of Daniel.

My personal takeaway from the entire book is the idea that God is always in control—which means that *we're* not. That's a tough thing for many of us to not only believe but also accept—especially those of us who like our power. In fact, I think one of the greatest illusions we buy in to is the illusion of control.

The book of Daniel focuses primarily on two characters. The first is Daniel, who was kidnapped from his home at a young age and taken captive by an enemy nation. He spent the first part of his life almost completely powerless. The other character is King Nebuchadnezzar, head of the nation who took Daniel captive. He seemed to have all the power and control any one human being could have.

In many ways, King Nebuchadnezzar had the life many of us think we want—a life of super success, endless riches, and plenty of power. It's the life many of us read about in magazines like *People* or *Sports Illustrated* and think, *I wouldn't mind giving that life a try.*

But access to all that power couldn't protect the king from problems. For instance,

> In the second year of his reign, Nebuchadnezzar had dreams; his mind was troubled and he could not sleep. So the king summoned the magicians, enchanters, sorcerers and astrologers to tell him what he had dreamed. (Dan. 2:1–2)

Isn't it interesting that the most powerful man in Babylon was so troubled that he could not sleep? I've had that happen to me when I was going through a difficult season in my life. It was usually due to an issue in my marriage or at work that I felt I had no control over. That lack of control made me quite anxious. I'm sure that was the problem for Nebuchadnezzar too.

For Nebuchadnezzar, the issue was his dreams. It's important that we apply a little context to this story so you can better understand what was going on with the king. In his day, it was widely accepted that gods spoke to the king through dreams and visions, so interpretation of these dreams was considered vital. Rulers had astrologers and advisors whose whole job was to help with dream interpretation. So when Nebuchadnezzar started having these disturbing dreams, he summoned his best interpreters and made sure they understood what was at stake:

> When they came in and stood before the king, he said to them, "I have had a dream that troubles me and I want to know what it means."
>
> Then the astrologers answered the king, "May the king live forever! Tell your servants the dream, and we will interpret it."
>
> The king replied to the astrologers, "This is what I have firmly decided: If you do not tell me what my dream was and interpret it, I will have you cut into pieces and your houses turned into piles of rubble. But if you tell me the dream and explain it, you will receive from me gifts and rewards and great honor. So tell me the dream and interpret it for me." (vv. 2–6)

Can you imagine the look on the astrologers' faces when they heard this? There's nothing like facing an impossible task first thing in the morning. And that's exactly what they told the king—that nobody could interpret a dream without knowing what the dream was.

Sounds reasonable, doesn't it? But Nebuchadnezzar wasn't feeling particularly reasonable—or merciful—on this particular day. He gave orders that the execution would proceed. In fact, he was going to execute all the wise men in the kingdom.

What was he so angry about? It doesn't really make sense until you consider what those dreams represented to Nebuchadnezzar. They were an unsettling reminder that there are some things even the most powerful man in the world cannot control. And when a power worshipper smashes his nose against the limits of his control, everyone suffers.

RED FLAGS ON THE SLIPPERY SLOPE

As I mentioned earlier in this chapter, I've struggled with power throughout my life. I like to be in charge. I like to have my way. I like to feel as though I have an influence on people and events. And I definitely don't like feeling helpless or inadequate. You might say I have some control issues, and they've affected my behavior all my life.

When I was very young, I pushed my weight around with my younger sister. As I grew, my control issues emerged with my friends, then later with my colleagues and my family. These days I often long to think I have power over outcomes.

And again, I think I'm pretty normal in this. We all like to feel we have a say in what happens in our lives. We all like to win, to make a difference, to do something significant, to have others look up to us. So how do we know whether our drive for significance has morphed into idolatry, that we're headed down the slippery slope and have begun to worship power?

In my own life I've identified two huge red flags.

Avoiding Failure

When any of us allow power to become an idol in our lives, we begin to get our very sense of identity from it. As a result, we'll do everything in our control to cover up any hint of weakness—whatever suggests we're not the commanding, in-charge kind of person we so desperately long to be.

For me this fleshes out in a variety of ways. My arguments with Brandi get longer and harder because I can't let myself give in. I'll lose my temper when situations and conversations make me feel inadequate. I'll explode when inanimate objects don't respond as I expect. (There's nothing more inspiring than a grown man yelling at a Weed eater!)

> A sure sign that my attitude toward power is out of whack is that I'll start doing everything I can to avoid failure.

And a sure sign that my attitude toward power is out of whack is that I'll start doing everything I can to avoid failure. The very prospect of not winning fills me with debilitating fear and anxiety. Sometimes I'll find myself pushing harder and more desperately to win at all costs. Other times I'll just freeze up and avoid taking any risks at all.

Almost two years ago I got the opportunity to write my first book, *Plan B*. Despite the fact that I felt prompted by God to write the book and my publisher had given me the green light, I still wrestled with actually getting it written. I procrastinated—a lot. I kept finding other things to do. Sitting down at the computer and writing was the very last thing I wanted to do.

Why was I having so much trouble? The main reason was that I was terrified of failing. I was haunted by the idea that my book would be rejected, that nobody would want to buy it, that I would be the laughingstock of the publishing community and lose the respect of my colleagues and friends and my congregation.

I'm not saying any of that would have happened, but the very possibility froze me in my tracks. Why was it so frightening? Because it involved the perceived loss of my influence and my identity as a valued and successful member of my community.

In other words, my writer's block was really a power issue in my life. Worshipping at the altar of power was essentially paralyzing me.

This can happen so easily in any life. We get to the point that our lives revolve around not failing instead of becoming and doing the things God calls us to do. We're so afraid of losing our identities as powerful people that we're unwilling to take the risks God wants us to take.

One of the biggest challenges we face with this form of idolatry is living apart from Christ's power in our lives. Paul recorded this insight in 2 Corinthians 12:9, when he recalled a word of the Lord in his own time of fear and anxiety: "But [God] said to me, 'My grace is sufficient for you, for my power is made perfect in weakness.' Therefore I will boast all the more gladly about my weaknesses, so that Christ's power may rest on me."

It's a decision we all must make—one that especially challenges those of us who lean in the direction of a power idol.

Do we want the perceived power that comes from avoiding failure?

Or do we want the authentic power that comes from Christ when we live and walk humbly with him?

Refusing Correction

Refusing correction is the second red flag that warns me I may be slipping into the worship of power. I'll also become impatient and rebellious toward the rules and processes that other people establish for me. It seems there's always a better way, and that better way is *my* way.

One of the sure ways of knowing that the cancer of power has crept into our hearts is the inability to admit we're wrong and a resistance to being held accountable. I'm telling you from firsthand experience, as power and influence increase in a person's life, there will be an increased temptation to live in isolation and shed accountability.

What happens is we start to think we're above everyone else.

- *I'm more important than they are.*
- *I have more responsibilities than they do.*
- *I know more than they do.*
- *Nobody had better cross me or question me!*

This dynamic was clearly at work in the story of King Nebuchadnezzar. He invited a group of advisors to speak into his life. But as soon as they gave him an answer he didn't want to hear, he decided he was going to kill them.

Allow me to be blunt for a moment. If you have a hard time taking correction from your spouse, a friend, a teacher, or a boss, you more than likely have some power issues. As Proverbs 15:12 puts it,

> *Mockers resent correction,*
> *so they avoid the wise.*

Part of the reason you don't consult the wise or listen to those around you is because if you're honest, you don't think there is anyone you know who has more wisdom than you. Besides, to let someone else correct you is to concede power to that person—a frightening prospect for someone who needs to feel powerful in order to feel that all is well.

THE ILLUSION OF CONTROL

I often picture control as a kind of circle in my life. The more power I gain, the larger the circle grows, and the more things in my life I have control over. Everyone realizes there are certain things they can control and certain things they can't control. But the more power we get, the farther we tend to believe our circle of control expands.

Maybe you think your circle encompasses your family or your career or your finances. Maybe you think if you had just a little more power, then your circle of control could even grow to include something like your future.

Sadly, that's just an illusion—and a dangerous one.

I've got a friend named Grant whom I met several years ago at a community meeting. I wouldn't say he's a close friend, but we have lunch from time to time, and for some reason I've felt God nudging me to pursue a relationship with him. To be honest, this isn't a nudge I've been real excited about because Grant isn't the most pleasant person to be around.

Several years ago I got a call in the middle of the night. When I finally stopped fumbling for the phone and looked at the caller ID, I saw it was Grant. As I said hello in my two-in-the-morning voice, I can't tell you how perplexed I was. I couldn't imagine any good reason for Grant to call me in the middle of the night. In fact, while he might have called my cell a few times to set up a meeting, I couldn't think of a single time he had ever called my home.

I could tell instantly that Grant was in rare form. He was crying, and his inability to put clear thoughts together tipped me off that he had been drinking. After about two minutes of ranting, he hung up. Concerned, I tried to call him back several times, but he never answered.

The next morning, Grant finally called back, and we arranged to meet that afternoon for lunch. Over sandwiches and soup, a very tired-looking Grant began to peel back the layers of his life.

To say Grant was a power-hungry control freak would be an understatement.

He was the founder and CEO of a local insurance company, and apparently he was known for being vicious and controlling in the workplace. The people who worked with him lived in constant fear of how he might react from day to day to their performance, which never seemed to meet his approval. He recounted story after story of how he had strategically positioned himself to gather larger and larger shares of power in his line of work.

At home it was more or less the same story. Grant had two children, a twelve-year-old daughter and a ten-year-old son. His relationship with both of them was damaged at best. His son had recently pleaded with him to not show up at any more of his baseball games because having Grant there was too much pressure. Apparently Grant had pulled his son out of the dugout at the last game and reamed him out. Grabbing the boy by the arm, he'd told the boy that he was an embarrassment and that if he wasn't going to try harder, he needed to just quit.

But Grant hadn't called me in the middle of the night because of his job or his kids. The real catalyst for our lunch meeting was that his wife, Cindy, had finally called it quits with him. Apparently he had gotten home around ten that evening and found her waiting for him. In a prerehearsed, nonemotional speech, she announced that she and the kids would be moving out come the weekend. "For fifteen years I've put up with your controlling, manipulative power plays, and I'm done," she said. "I'm done with the emotional abuse. I'm done being a pawn in your game. I'm done."

> The truth is, we're never as powerful as we want to think we are. And when we insist on worshipping at the altar of this empty promise, we set ourselves up for an inevitable comedown.

Grant's pursuit of power over his life had pushed the people closest to him farther and farther away. In his desire to widen his circle of control, he had ruined his chance at emotional intimacy with the people he supposedly cared the most about. He had fallen for the empty promises that trip so many of us up—the lie that more power will expand the circle of our control.

Every once in a while an event takes place like me with my elders or Nebuchadnezzar with his dreams or Grant with his family or Paul and his affair. Then we suddenly realize what I think we all somehow know but hate to admit: that our circles of control are much smaller than we ever imagined. While power may puff up the *illusion* of control, it does not, in fact, equal more control.

The truth is, we're never as powerful as we want to think we are. And when we insist on worshipping at the altar of this empty promise, we set ourselves up for an inevitable comedown.

THE ALTERNATIVE TO A POWER TRIP

Let's get back to our story in Daniel. When several of Nebuchadnezzar's advisors were unable to interpret his dreams, the king decided to kill *all* of his advisors—and our buddy Daniel was one of them. Fortunately, Daniel had a much better understanding of power than Nebuchadnezzar did. He chose to go to the Source of all real power.

> When Arioch, the commander of the king's guard, had gone out to put to death the wise men of Babylon, Daniel spoke to him with wisdom and tact. He asked the king's officer, "Why did the king issue such a harsh decree?" Arioch then explained the matter to Daniel. At this, Daniel went in to the king and asked for time, so that he might interpret the dream for him.
>
> Then Daniel returned to his house and explained the matter to his friends Hananiah, Mishael and Azariah. He urged them to plead for mercy from the God of heaven concerning this mystery, so that he and his friends might not be executed with the rest of the wise men of Babylon. During the night the mystery was revealed to Daniel in a vision. (2:14–19)

What a brave moment—for Daniel to step in and say, "I believe my God can do this." And during that night, God answered. God showed up and revealed the mystery to Daniel.

The story goes on to tell of how Daniel explained the dream to Nebuchadnezzar. The king not only canceled the execution order but actually got on his knees and praised Daniel's God, the God of heaven. Just for that moment, the king realized as a result of this experience that his worship of power was in fact a dead end. It was not going to give him what he had hoped. Power was in fact an empty promise that had left him hurting and desperate.

Nebuchadnezzar actually had an opportunity to change his power-grabbing ways. Unfortunately he didn't do that. He embarked on his power trips again and again, punishing anyone who stood up to him, until God was forced to bring him down. And what a downfall that was. Nebuchadnezzar went crazy, had all his power stripped away from him, and lived like an animal in the fields for seven years. It took that much for Nebuchadnezzar to humble himself and turn away from the empty promise of power.

What a contrast between this stubborn, power-hungry king and his captive-turned-advisor Daniel. From the beginning, Daniel modeled a completely different approach to power. Just listen to his prayer:

> *Praise be to the name of God for ever and ever;*
> *wisdom and power are his.*
> *He changes times and seasons;*
> *he deposes kings and raises up others.*
> *He gives wisdom to the wise*
> *and knowledge to the discerning. (vv. 20–21)*

I love the fact that Daniel was not pursuing or acknowledging his own power. In fact, he was doing the exact opposite. He was simply praising God and recognizing that all power belongs to God. And in so doing, he pointed the way to what can happen when we stop pushing at the circles of our own control and make room for the God of all power to do his work in our lives.

King David wrote about this very thing in Psalm 91:

> Whoever dwells in the shelter of the Most High
> will rest in the shadow of the Almighty.
> I will say of the LORD, "He is my refuge and my fortress,
> my God, in whom I trust." (vv. 1–2)

When we focus our thoughts on magnifying God instead of ourselves, we come to dwell in his shadow. And while the shadows of our problems, issues, and conflicts seem oppressive and overwhelming, the shadow of our God opens up a whole new world to us.

A world of rest.

EVENING AND MORNING

The ancient Hebrew mind-set about the structure of a day was very different from the way we look at it today. According to Mosaic law, a day actually started at sunset instead of sunrise.

That's quite the opposite from what most of us imagine, isn't it? Don't you think about the day starting at sunrise when you're getting up and entering into the circumstances and events of your day?

But look at this example in Genesis: "And there was evening, and there was morning—the fourth day" (Gen. 1:19). The assumption is that the day begins with evening, not the morning.

I love this thought, and while you may not think it really matters, think about the implications behind this idea. To me, it helps put the whole power issue into perspective.

The day doesn't start when *you* get up and get going, for this day is not dependent on your thoughts, actions, and participation. Instead, it begins in the evening, when *you* wind down and go to bed. And while you sleep, God keeps watch. He does not sleep. (We may not like to admit it, but the universe gets along just fine without us.)

If this is true during the nighttime, it's true during the daytime too. Which means you can let go of your stress, your problems, your anxiety and insecurity. You don't have to be in charge, because you have a God who's got your back. He'll take care of everything, and there's only one thing you have to do.

You have to surrender.

NOT AS I WILL

With tears welling up in his eyes, my friend Paul, the former senator, told me about a night where things began to change and he felt God's power in his life like never before:

"It was just a couple of weeks after my story had broken and was circulating around the country. I was staying at a friend's house. The house was for sale and was completely empty except for a few remaining pieces of furniture. I was literally lying facedown on the floor crying out to God. I would fall asleep praying and crying and would wake up only to start crying again. I couldn't get off the floor. I went from an arrogant man trying to dominate Capitol Hill to a broken, surrendered man facedown in a puddle of his own tears. I was finally ready to surrender.

"You're going to replace the idol of power with something. I had to replace the trappings of power with God's love and mercy. It's not the same feeling as those false gods, but he gives you something I didn't get from power. I got true acceptance, forgiveness, and the opportunity to live my life for him. I didn't know what grace and mercy really [were] until my little world and all of my idols came crashing down."

It's interesting to me that Paul finally found what he was looking for in the most powerless moment of his life. In this moment he was permanently hindered, yet permanently fulfilled. He was humbled, yet restored when he gave up on his power god and surrendered to the God of power and might.

You don't have to be in charge, because you have a God who's got your back. He'll take care of everything, and there's only one thing you have to do. You have to surrender.

We see the same paradox in the story of Daniel. Nebuchadnezzar seemed to be the one with all the power. He was the one making decisions and ordering people around. And yet we see him as troubled, stressed, and full of fear. Then Daniel, who seemingly had no power, no control, simply surrendered to God and in doing so saved lives.

Surrender was the turning point in someone else's life as well. Remember this scene with Jesus in the Garden of Gethsemane?

Then Jesus went with his disciples to a place called Gethsemane, and he said to them, "Sit here while I go over there and pray." He took Peter and the two sons of Zebedee along with him, and he began to be sorrowful and troubled. Then he said to them, "My soul is overwhelmed with sorrow to the point of death. Stay here and keep watch with me."

Going a little farther, he fell with his face to the ground and prayed, "My Father, if it is possible, may this cup be taken from me. Yet not as I will, but as you will."

Then he returned to his disciples and found them sleeping. "Couldn't you men keep watch with me for one hour?" he asked Peter. "Watch and pray so that you will not fall into temptation. The spirit is willing, but the flesh is weak."

He went away a second time and prayed, "My Father, if it is

not possible for this cup to be taken away unless I drink it, may your will be done." (Matt. 26:36–42)

That's a prayer of surrender. "Not as I will, but as you will." That's a "Here's me—here's all of me" prayer. *Here's me giving up my desire for power and control, my right to have my own way*—that's what Jesus was praying.

Ironically, this may be the most powerful moment in Jesus' ministry.

It's more powerful than feeding the multitudes.

It's more powerful than healing the blind and deaf.

It's more powerful than the winds and waves ceasing with his spoken word.

It's more powerful than when he called Lazarus out of the grave.

There is a life-changing, identity-forming power available when we're willing to say to God, "I give up my drive for power, and I surrender." When we finally get it through our heads that there is a God and we're not him.

It's something worth thinking about. Where do you need to say, "Not as I will, but as you will"? Where do you need to push back against this idolatry and make your surrender?

A situation at work?

A circumstance in your marriage?

An issue with your kids or your parents or your siblings?

Something with a treasured friend?

GIVE UP YOUR GRIP

Not too long ago I took my three boys to an amusement park in Indiana. The summer was coming to a close, and I thought it would be a great way to end the season. My oldest son, Jett, is getting old enough—and, finally, tall enough—to ride a few roller coasters with me. That's something I love to do, and I was excited about doing it with my son.

He wasn't all that excited, though—not at first. It took me awhile to talk him into getting on the park's biggest wooden roller coaster. With his hand clamped on my leg and his eyes shut tightly, he made it through the first ride. In fact, I talked him into riding it with me a few more times, and we really had fun together.

We went on with our day and rode some other rides. Then, as we were leaving the park that night, I suggested, "Jett, why don't you ride the 'big one' with me one more time."

He was a lot more confident now. "Yeah."

"This time I've got a surprise for you," I said. "This time we're going to ride in the front seat of the coaster. That's the best seat of all."

He looked uncertain, but I just knew he was going to enjoy this. So we waited in line, and the moment came when we were finally belted in to the front seat. As the coaster started to move, I looked at Jett and said, "Buddy, there's one more thing I forgot to tell you. When you sit in the front seat, it's a rule that you have to keep your hands up the entire time."

He looked at me with big eyes. "Really, Dad?"

Trying not to smile, I quickly replied with, "Yes, son, it's a rule."

So he raised his hands in the air, determined to follow the "rule." As the roller coaster slowly cranked up the hill he had his hands high in the sky. But as soon as we crested the top of the hill and started the plunge, he grabbed onto the bar for dear life. When we reached the bottom, his hands went back up. But whenever we reached another curve or dip, his hands came down. It was quite entertaining to watch.

As we were getting off the coaster, I turned to Jett and said, "Well, what did you think?"

Without hesitation he said, "Dad, I didn't like that at all."

"You didn't?"

"No, I don't like having my hands up."

Then Jett said something I'll never forget. He said, "When I had my hands up, I didn't feel safe."

I think it's interesting that the international sign of surrender is lifting your hands in the air. You can go anywhere in the world, and if you lift your hands in the air it means the same thing: I surrender.

I don't know that anyone enjoys the process of surrender. It means voluntarily giving up power and control, and that's a scary thing for most of us. Surrendering doesn't feel safe. And yet we see it was a turning point for Daniel and Jesus and countless others, and it can be a turning point in your life today.

One of my favorite verses in the Bible is Psalm 46:10: "Be still, and know that I am God."

The Hebrew word for "be still" literally means "let go." It tells us to cease striving at the level of human effort.

Be still and let go of your own understanding.

Be still and let go of your own human effort.

Be still and let go of your desire for more power.

Be still and let go of your need to control outcomes.

Be still.

Be still and be reminded that you are finite . . . but God is infinite.

Be still and let God be God in the most intimate places of your life. Because in the end, that's the only power that will change anything.

CHAPTER SIX
MONEY ALWAYS WANTS TO BE MORE THAN MONEY

It was February 15 and exactly 3:02 in the morning in Kolkata, India. I should have been asleep. But at home in Nashville it was only 2:32 in the afternoon, so my body was a bit confused. Besides, my mind was wrestling with a question.

It was my fourth day leading a team of people from my church on a mission trip to work in the slums of India, my third trip in just two years. But what I had seen and experienced that day had once again shocked me as if it were the first time my eyes had been opened to injustice.

We'd spent most of the day visiting shacks to see if there was anything we could do to assist the residents of the Khalpar slum, where we were working to start a school and feeding center. One particular dwelling we walked up to was even more ragged than the average shack in this slum. It was actually just a series of ripped sheets that had been taped together and propped up by six or seven rickety-looking sticks.

The family who lived there invited us in. They were cooking something in a pot over the fire. I sat there with my team of three or four and our translator packed into this tiny makeshift tent with the husband, wife, and three children who called it home. A makeshift bed in the corner consisted of a throwaway piece of plywood covered with several layers of muddy, frazzled blankets. In the corners of the tent were small piles of dingy-looking clothes—not enough to pack for a weekend getaway for my three boys, but all the clothes they owned.

I asked the father what he did for a living. The translator rephrased the question for me, listened to the answer, then told me, "He pulls a rickshaw when he can get work, but it's pretty inconsistent." The translator went on to explain that this was a very physically demanding job with few breaks for the workers during the day. The father would work three or four days a week, making close to fifty cents a day.

I then asked what the mother did and was told she was a servant for a wealthy family in Kolkata. Every day she walked two hours to get to the home where she worked. After a full day of cleaning clothes, mopping floors, and doing other backbreaking household chores, she walked the two hours back home. She also made less than fifty cents a day.

Their kids were extraordinarily well behaved. I would imagine they'd been given the same life-threatening speeches I give my kids when guests come to our house, but for some reason these kids actually listened. The youngest, a little girl about three years old, actually climbed into my lap. Her brown skin and dark hair complemented the bluest eyes, and the dirt on her face couldn't hide the fact that she was one of the prettiest children I had ever seen.

In an attempt to get small talk going in what was a bit of an awkward situation, someone in the group asked what was cooking over the fire. The husband, noticeably disturbed, went into a lengthy conversation with the translator.

Eventually the translator said, "The father says they're eating dirt cookies tonight."

I quickly responded with, "What's that?"

She explained to me that these "dirt cookies" were literally what they sounded like—dirt mixed with a little oil. She went on to explain that while they had little nutritional value, these dirt cookies would temporarily dull the family's hunger pains.

My heart sank. I looked into the blue eyes of the little girl sitting in my lap and lost it.

I remember looking toward the back of the tent and away from the group as if I had been distracted by something or was trying to find something. The fact was I was trying to hide the tears that had started to stream down my face. I prayed, "Dear God, please allow me to hold it together right now," but my entire chest was starting to convulse from the pent-up emotion. I thought, *God, how is this possible? My kids fight over whether or not they have to eat all of their vegetables and whine about why we have to eat spaghetti tonight when we just had it three weeks ago. These malnourished kids are literally eating dirt.*

We hung out with this family for another twenty minutes or so and learned they were the only Christians in this particular slum. Their genuine love for each other and their kids was clear. Their oldest son, Balek, who walked with a limp, was in fact not their biological son. They had found him in a trash heap years before, probably discarded because of his partial paralysis. They had taken him home and were raising him as their own.

I left that little tent in a state of shock—and not just because of horrific poverty. What really amazed me was the sense of peace that filled the place. Despite working so hard for next to nothing and having to eat dirt to simply stay alive, that family had a contagious, undeniable sense of calm about them. It truly surpassed all understanding.

A question began bothering me as we rode back to the dorms where we were staying. It invaded my mind much like the fly that won't leave you alone at the Fourth of July picnic. It annoyed me and woke me up in the middle of the night, when I desperately just wanted to sleep. I kept wondering why that poverty-stricken, dirt-cookie-eating family had so much more peace than me, my friends, and my family, who have access to more money than the Khalpar Christians could ever imagine?

There is zero correlation between money and true peace. Zero.

Why did that family have more peace than most of you reading this book right now?

Why?

I pondered that question for a long time. And the glorious, liberating truth that finally came to me was this:

There is zero correlation between money and true peace.

Zero.

You can try—as so many others have—to squeeze one ounce of peace from the stacks of money and stuff you own, but you'll fail. You won't find it there. There is no greater empty promise than this lie that has tricked millions and millions of people of every nation, race, age, and tax bracket.

The empty promise that money will buy you anything you really need.

IT SNEAKS UP ON YOU

It's interesting that Jesus talked more about money than he did about heaven, hell, and prayer combined. Was it because he was fixated on it? No, but he knew we would be. He knew there is a certain allure to wealth and possessions, a vicious grip that human beings find hard to shake. I think Jesus also understood that the issue of money is especially problematic because the worship of money is tricky to identify.

One reason for this, I believe, is that it expresses itself so many different ways. One person may spend like crazy in an attempt to feel worthwhile, while someone else may be super frugal and sock away every penny into investments—for the same reason. The behavior may be completely different. But if both people are using money to make them feel safe and in control, there's a good chance they're making an idol of it.

I once heard a pastor ask, "Which of the following statements creates more anxiety in your heart: 'There is no God' or, 'There is no money in the bank'?" His point? The idolatry of money is not only the love of money, but excessive anxiety over it. And let's face it; we're all susceptible to feeling anxious about our finances. Few of us can go through this world without looking to money to give us what only God can.

Another thing that makes this empty promise extremely difficult to identify is the fact that very few of us think we actually "love wealth." We're not likely to believe money is an idol for us. Greed and materialism—both aspects of the money idol—camouflage themselves quite effectively.

How? Most often by association. Without even realizing it we align ourselves with a particular socioeconomic bracket.

We shop with people in that bracket.

We go to movies with people in that bracket.

We live next to people in that bracket.

We attend church with people in that bracket.

And we almost always compare ourselves to people in our bracket.

We don't compare ourselves with the rest of the world. We live and work in our own little brackets and let them determine our ideas of what is normal, what is enough, and what is necessary. "I'm not greedy," we tell ourselves. "Look at them. Look at the remodeling job they just did. Look at the money she spends on clothes. Look at what he spends on his yard."

This kind of thinking hit me hard one morning while I was driving my boys to school. It suddenly occurred to me that the truck I was driving was a piece of junk. At the time it was ten years old and was beginning to have a few issues, but until that moment I had been satisfied with it. But I started to think, *Pete, what are you doing driving this truck? What you need is a new four-door jeep. A black four-wheel-drive jeep that's really tricked out.*

And I really would need one of those . . . if I lived out in the country in a place where it snows three hundred days out of the year and my house was built on top of a craggy rock pile. Truth is, I drive my kids to school on roads that are smooth as a glass table. What am I gonna say—"Better kick on the four-by-four to get through this pothole starting to form in the street"? If there's anything men can be counted on for, it's overdoing it!

This little conversation went on in my head for a few minutes, and then I felt God's Spirit convict me. *Really, Pete? You* need *a new jeep? How is it that your truck, which gets you where you need to go, is suddenly inadequate? Why must you have something newer, nicer, better?*

I accepted that conviction as I recognized I was buying into the empty promise that somehow a new vehicle was going to bring me happiness or significance.

That was, until we arrived in the drop-off line at the school and I saw the guy directly in front of me was driving a beautiful, black, shiny BMW 118d convertible. What a beautiful car. There was a bit of drool hanging off my lip as that guy's two kids climbed out of the back and shuffled into school.

I sat there thinking, *I'm not greedy. Look at that guy—he's greedy. I just want a jeep, and he's sporting around in a new Beamer convertible.*

Be careful. This empty promise will sneak up on you. We're reminded of that in Jesus' teaching.

Someone in the crowd said to him, "Teacher, tell my brother to divide the inheritance with me."

Jesus replied, "Man, who appointed me a judge or an arbiter between you?" Then he said to them, "Watch out! Be on your guard against all kinds of greed; life does not consist in an abundance of possessions." (Luke 12:13–15)

Notice the strong lesson. "Watch out!" Jesus warns. "Be on guard." He *knew* how tricky this idol can be.

Greed is a sin that, unlike many others, comes with all kinds of yellow caution tape in the Bible—precisely because it's so hard for us to spot in our lives. You won't find Jesus saying, "Watch out! Make sure you're not committing adultery." He doesn't have to. If you're sleeping with someone who isn't your spouse, you know it.

But greed isn't like that. It's inherently self-deceptive. Money is something many of us just don't handle well. It seems to amplify our selfish tendencies, almost like adding a toxin to the soul. And our materialistic culture doesn't help matters. We need to realize that simply breathing the air of our society means that we probably struggle with this issue to one degree or another.

Jesus was not vague about the danger of this idol. One time he said, "No one can serve two masters. Either you will hate the one and love the other, or you will be devoted to the one and despise the other. You cannot serve both God and money" (Matt. 6:24).

So let's approach this whole issue from the standpoint of, "This could easily be me. I'm going to keep my heart open to the fact that maybe God wants to point some things out to me today."

IT'S NEVER JUST MONEY

I've had to learn the hard way that money never wants to be just money in my life. It's always trying to position and manipulate itself into becoming something more. In fact, what I discover most often is that it lures me into falling for three illusions. Let's take a look at them.

Illusion #1: More Money Will Give Me More Security

Look at this sentence from a letter the apostle Paul wrote to his younger colleague Timothy and the church he was leading in Ephesus:

> Command those who are rich in this present world not to be arrogant nor to put their hope in wealth, which is so uncertain, but to put their hope in God, who richly provides us with everything for our enjoyment. (1 Tim. 6:17)

The people Paul was writing about were Christians who sang the songs, showed up at the temple, and memorized the Scriptures. Many were believers who had faced death for their faith in Christ. But still he had to remind them, "Hey, as time goes by, don't start to buy into the empty promise of money. Don't fall into thinking it can provide you security."

How much money do you think you need to be totally financially secure? I think the answer to that question is the same for all of us. More than you currently have.

Have you ever had a conversation with yourself that went something like this? "If I could make fifty-five thousand dollars a year instead of forty-five thousand, we would be set. We would finally be secure and not have to fight or worry about money."

Of course all the people who make fifty-five thousand a year are saying, "If we just made *sixty-five* thousand, then we would finally feel secure and not have to worry about money."

How much money do you think you need to be totally financially secure? I think the answer to that question is the same for all of us.

More than you currently have.

I recently read a fascinating article in the *Atlantic* based on a Boston College study of the very rich (those worth twenty-five million or more). This article really reveals how money can undermine the very things we need most—dependence on God, trusting relationships, meaningful work, purpose and direction—and how it can skew the way we look at life. One of the individuals they interviewed in the article,

> the heir to an enormous fortune, says that what matters most to him is his Christianity, and that his greatest aspiration is "to love the Lord, my family, and my friends." He also reports that he wouldn't feel financially secure until he had $1 billion in the bank.[1]

Proverbs 18:11 says,

> *The wealth of the rich is their fortified city;*
> *they imagine it a wall too high to scale.*

Did you see the key word in that verse? It's *imagine*. They imagine it. It's not real.

It's not just the rich who fall for this illusion, of course. But the more money we accrue, the more tempted we may be to think it gives us a security it can never provide.

Material wealth cannot provide emotional or spiritual security. Ask any "poor little rich kid" who grew up with things instead of love and attention. It cannot even provide material security. Ask any victim of a house fire . . . or a Ponzi scheme . . . or a tornado.

No wonder Jesus insisted,

> Do not store up for yourselves treasures on earth, where moths and vermin destroy, and where thieves break in and steal. But

store up for yourselves treasures in heaven, where moths and vermin do not destroy, and where thieves do not break in and steal. (Matt. 6:19–20)

Illusion #2: More Money Will Give Me More Peace and Happiness

You've heard the old cliché that "money can't buy happiness." Recent research indicates it's more than just a cliché. MSN Money columnist Brent Kessel wrote,

> Richard A. Easterlin, an economics professor at the University of Southern California and a former Guggenheim Fellow, has done extensive research that "found no significant relationship between happiness and time over a period in which GDP (gross domestic product) per capita grew by one-third, from 1972 to 1991." . . .
>
> "Two economists, Andrew Oswald at Warwick University and David Blanchflower from Dartmouth, found that there's no improvement in happiness in either the U.S. or Great Britain as income rises," Easterlin explains. "If you follow a single person over time as they move from lower income to higher income, you find no increase in their happiness."[2]

Ecclesiastes 5:10 says,

> *Whoever loves money never has enough;*
> *whoever loves wealth is never satisfied with their income.*

It's true, isn't it? There are few things that we worry about the way we worry about money. We worry about how to make more, how to make it go further, how to invest it, how to save it, how to spend it, and how to protect it. And we easily buy into the illusion that what we need to keep us from worrying about money is more money.

So we keep getting more and more money, and what do we end up thinking about?

More money.

And yet somehow we keep falling for the lie that if we had more, we'd be happier and more satisfied.

Max Lucado vividly depicted the fallout from this illusion:

Come with me to the most populated prison in the world. The facility has more inmates than bunks. More prisoners than plates. More residents than resources.

Come with me to the world's most oppressive prison. Just ask the inmates; they will tell you. They are overworked and underfed. Their walls are bare and bunks are hard.

No prison is so populated, no prison so oppressive, and, what's more, no prison is so permanent. Most inmates never leave. They never escape. They never get released. They serve a life sentence in this overcrowded, underprovisioned facility.

The name of the prison? You'll see it over the entrance. Rainbowed over the gate are four cast-iron letters that spell out its name:

W-A-N-T.

The prison of want. You've seen her prisoners. They are "in want." They want something. They want something bigger. Nicer. Faster. Thinner. They want.

They don't want much, mind you. They want just one thing. One new job. One new car. One new house. One new spouse. They don't want much. They want just one.[3]

Jesus once wanted to talk about this tendency even very smart human beings have to fool themselves about money and think it provides satisfaction. So in his typical master-teacher fashion, he told a story.

The ground of a certain rich man yielded an abundant harvest. He thought to himself, "What shall I do? I have no place to store my crops."

Then he said, "This is what I'll do. I will tear down my barns and build bigger ones, and there I will store my surplus grain. And I'll say to myself, 'You have plenty of grain laid up for many years. Take life easy; eat, drink and be merry.'"

But God said to him, "You fool! This very night your life will be demanded from you. Then who will get what you have prepared for yourself?"

This is how it will be with whoever stores up things for themselves but is not rich toward God." (Luke 12:16–21)

Enough will never be enough. You're kidding yourself if you think that a little more money—or a lot—will bring you more peace, satisfaction, or happiness.

When Jesus said, "It is better to give than to receive" he wasn't just giving us a quotation we could use on greeting cards at Christmas. He really meant it. You'll actually like your life more, you'll actually have more peace, if you spend more time thinking about how you can give than how you can get.

Illusion #3: More Money Will Make Me More Generous

My wife, Brandi, and I have always enjoyed hosting small-group Bible studies in our home. Over the fifteen years we've been married, we've almost always had a group that met regularly in our house. I'll never forget something that happened some time ago in one of those groups.

At the time we were serving in Morgantown, Kentucky, and our group was made up of married couples and singles. One of them was a single woman who worked at a local factory. I'll call her Peggy.

On this particular night we were talking about generosity. She had remained quiet for most of the conversation but spoke up during prayer requests at the end.

She said, "Pete, it's no secret to most of you that I play the lottery on a regular basis. I would like to ask you and the group to pray that I win the Kentucky Powerball this week. It's up to forty-seven million, and if I won that kind of money, I guarantee you I would give a lot of it away."

That request put me in a difficult position. I wasn't even sure if as a pastor I was allowed to pray for someone to win the lottery. I asked her if she would tithe on the winnings and she said yes. So I prayed and I prayed hard. But after the meeting finished I felt prompted to explore the issue a little further.

I asked her, "Peggy, do you give any of your money away right now? Do you tithe or give to any causes or individuals or anything?"

She thought for a second and said, "No, not really."

I asked, "Between you and me, how much money do you make a year?"

She said, "I make about twenty-one thousand dollars a year."

"Peggy, what in the world makes you think that you would be generous with forty-seven million if you're not generous with twenty-one thousand?"

She sat there for a second but

When Jesus said, "It is better to give than to receive" he wasn't just giving us a quotation we could use on greeting cards at Christmas. He really meant it. You'll actually like your life more, you'll actually have more peace, if you spend more time thinking about how you can give than how you can get.

really had no response. And I didn't push the matter because, to be honest, there are times when I find myself thinking the same way she did.

This may be one of the greatest illusions about money. We think the only reason we're not generous is because things are too tight right now and we don't make a lot. We think, *When I make more money I'm going to start being generous.*

The trouble is, it doesn't usually work that way.

A number of recent surveys have indicated that lower-income people actually give a higher percentage of their income away than wealthy people do.[4] The more you get, the harder it is for you to be generous. So if you can't be generous when you make twenty-one thousand, you will likely not be generous when you make forty-one thousand. If you're not generous with forty-one thousand, you likely won't be generous with a hundred and forty thousand.

If you can't be generous with what you have now, you will probably never be generous with more.

THE TENSION

So what do you think? Is it possible that money has become an idol for you? Is it possible that you're relying on it to give you something that only God can give you? Here are a couple of questions to help you find clarity:

- Do you have plenty of money in the bank but no peace in your heart?
- Do you often find yourself saying (or thinking), "If I had this much, then I would be satisfied"?
- Do you spend more time thinking about what you do not have than you spend thanking God for what you do have?

And especially:

- Does your desire for more or your fear of not having enough often impede your desire to be generous?

Jesus focused on this last question in his encounter with a gentleman we often refer to as the rich young ruler:

> A certain ruler asked [Jesus], "Good teacher, what must I do to inherit eternal life?"
>
> "Why do you call me good?" Jesus answered. "No one is good—except God alone. You know the commandments: 'You shall not commit adultery, you shall not murder, you shall not steal, you shall not give false testimony, honor your father and mother.'"
>
> "All these I have kept since I was a boy," he said.
>
> When Jesus heard this, he said to him, "You still lack one thing. Sell everything you have and give to the poor, and you will have treasure in heaven. Then come, follow me."
>
> When he heard this, he became very sad, because he was very wealthy. Jesus looked at him and said, "How hard it is for the rich to enter the kingdom of God! Indeed, it is easier for a camel to go through the eye of a needle than for someone who is rich to enter the kingdom of God." (Luke 18:18–25)

Do you see what's going on in this story? This rich young man wasn't making the connection between his attitude toward his possessions and his relationship with God. He was letting his money hold him back from experiencing the freedom of depending on his heavenly Father instead of on his wealth. Jesus wanted him to experience the reality that while receiving can be good, the greatest benefit comes in loosening our clutch on what we believe is ours and daring to give it away.

That's a lesson I believe we all need when it comes to our money and our lives. We need to learn the joy of letting go. In fact, we probably need to learn it over and over again, to counteract the temptations of idolatry in our lives.

There are times in my life I feel like I'm supposed to give money to something, and a huge string of questions rushes to my mind:

- Is this really a good cause?
- What about my kids' college education?
- Will they manage this money correctly?
- Should I be saving for retirement instead of giving to this cause?
- What if my car breaks down and I need money for an emergency repair on the engine?

We're taught by very wise people to save, save, save. And saving leaves less room to give, give, give and puts me in a position where my first thought about new money is saving versus giving.

Now, I'm not advocating a careless strategy to money. I'm not saying you shouldn't have savings or investigate whom you're giving to. But maybe, just maybe, it's not our responsibility to know exactly how our money is spent. Maybe God is more interested in our hearts than our financial strategies. Maybe we need to learn to let go of our money and trust God with it.

The Bible says that the rich young ruler went away feeling sorrowful. But Jesus was even more sorrowful because he knew what divine joy and divine purpose the young man was forfeiting.

His ultimate problem was not that he *had* riches. His problem was that he *trusted* in his riches. That affected what he did with his money. Because he put his faith in money instead of in God to see him through, he was not able to use his gifts the way Jesus called him to use them. And he missed out on the security and satisfaction and freedom that come from putting his faith where it really belongs.

Jesus could not have been clearer. This tension will be there all of your life. Everything inside of you will want to turn to money to feed your God-given desires for security and peace and happiness. Everything in you will urge you to hold your money close instead of giving it away.

Don't fall for it. It's a trap.

In fact, the only way I know how to fight back against allowing money to become an idol, the only way I know how to break the greedy pattern of get, get, get in my life, is the one Jesus taught us and modeled for us again and again.

The healthy way to handle money—and any other potential idol in our lives—is to give, give, give, trusting God to provide what we really need.

CHAPTER SEVEN
RELIGION LIES

Trevor is a good friend of mine who has been a pastor for almost thirty years. We met for lunch one day recently, and I noticed that Trevor was looking a little frayed around the edges. In fact, he looked exhausted.

When I inquired about his tired appearance, I saw tears well up in his eyes.

"Pete, do you ever wonder how much is enough? How good is good enough?"

I didn't really have an answer to that. I just nodded to show I was listening as Trevor went on. "Most of my ministry has been spent living in fear that I'm not good enough for God. From day to day I question whether or not he really loves me. And the harder I try, the more I feel like I'm failing."

NEVER ENOUGH

My friend Trevor is hardly alone in his struggle. I think many of us wrestle with this constant need to please God, to earn his love and acceptance with our good deeds. I call this the spiritual treadmill, a condition that causes us to work harder and harder and never feel like we're really making any progress.

How do you know if you're stuck on the spiritual treadmill? Here are some questions to ask yourself:

- In the back of your mind, do you suspect that the more you obey God, the more he will love you?
- Even though you "know better," does part of you believe being a good, moral person will increase your chances of getting into heaven?
- Do you think that being obedient to God should increase your chances at better health, more wealth, more power and control?
- Do you find yourself regularly battling uncertainty about your standing before God?

Our lives tell the tale over and over again: religion can be just another empty promise. Whenever we end up putting our faith in our religion rather than in the living God—that's an idol.

The spiritual treadmill is driven by the assumption that *If I can do just a little more for God, then I'll know he loves me or accepts me.* This mind-set leads us into believing that freedom will exist at the next level of spiritual attainment. The problem is, once we reach our goal, the spiritual bar gets raised. We always end up falling short and usually feel the need to once again make up for our failures. So we try and try and never seem to get anywhere.

Our lives tell the tale over and over again: religion can be just another empty promise. Whenever we end up putting our faith in our religion rather than in the living God—that's an idol.

This most often occurs when people rely on the rightness of their doctrines or the rightness of their actions for their standing with God rather than on God himself and his grace. It is a subtle but deadly mistake.

The thing is, religion tends to sniff out the insecurities that we wrestle with and that lure us in. The religion idol whispers, "If you would just

- give more;
- show up more;
- serve more;
- pray more;
- read more;
- memorize more;
- preach more;
- evangelize more;
- sing more;

then, and only then, will you be safe. Then will God love you. At the very least, if you do all this, he'll love you more."

Jesus pointed out this very fallacy to his friend Martha one day when he was visiting her and her sister Mary:

As Jesus and his disciples were on their way, he came to a village where a woman named Martha opened her home to him. She had a sister called Mary, who sat at the Lord's feet listening to what he said. But Martha was distracted by all the preparations that had to be made. She came to him and asked, "Lord, don't you care that my sister has left me to do the work by myself? Tell her to help me!"

"Martha, Martha," the Lord answered, "you are worried and upset about many things, but few things are needed—or indeed only one. Mary has chosen what is better, and it will not be taken away from her." (Luke 10:38–42)

Martha, it seems, was trying to find her identity in *doing* for the Lord instead of just *being* with the Lord like her sister Mary. And Jesus gently set her straight, telling her in no uncertain terms that what he valued most of all was not her service but her heart.

I tend to have the same problem Martha did. I'm always falling for the lie that God is more pleased with me when I'm doing something for him instead of just trying to be with him. When I get to thinking that way, I'm in danger of making an idol out of religion.

I believe it was the great reformer Martin Luther who insightfully suggested that religion is the default mode of the human heart. That's certainly true for me and so many people I know. We lapse way too easily into that mind-set where the church becomes more important than Christ. Where ritual becomes more important than relationship. Where the security of crossing off a certain religious activity becomes more important than your neighbor. And so it goes, on and on. That's the danger.

Such religion rests on the premise that God is by nature inclined to withhold his love, but that if we submit to the system we might earn his love . . . someday. Ironically, we fall into this empty promise willingly because our hearts long for love and security, and somewhere along the way most of us have convinced ourselves that all love is conditional.

So we hop on the spiritual treadmill and we run. We run and

run and run. But the more we run, the more exhausted we become. Every day we wonder, wish, and hope we've done enough.

It's all so sad . . . and so unnecessary.

Because the truth is, what you do *with* Jesus has always been more important than what you do *for* Jesus.

NOT THE FIRST

As a pastor I love the book of Acts. Not only does it provide a fascinating portrait of the highs and lows of the early church; it also reassures me that my church is a lot more normal than I think. And the book of Acts is also a rich source of insight into the early church's struggle with making religion a god.

I think we often forget that most of the early Christians were religious people *before* they began following Christ. They had spent most of their lives following the religious customs of their Jewish faith. When they converted to Christianity and pledged to follow the way of Jesus, many of them struggled with mixing and often elevating their Jewish customs to an unhealthy place.

In Acts 15, for instance, we read,

> Certain people came down from Judea to Antioch and were teaching the believers: "Unless you are circumcised, according to the custom taught by Moses, you cannot be saved." This brought Paul and Barnabas into sharp dispute and debate with them. So Paul and Barnabas were appointed, along with some other believers, to go up to Jerusalem to see the apostles and elders about this question. (vv. 1–2)

Now, I can just imagine a group of Gentiles sitting in some kind of first-century new members' class talking about their new faith, when the Jewish leader says, "Oh, just one more thing. You're all going to need to be circumcised."

"Why would we do that?"

"Well, that's what we do. It's what we've always done. It's the fundamental sign of the covenant between God and us."

"We thought Jesus was the fundamental sign. We thought we just had to believe in him."

"You do. But we also need you to do this one last thing if you want to be saved."

I don't think I have to explain to you why this might not have gone over too well with the Gentiles.

RELIGION ALWAYS ADDS

What was happening in that Acts 15 story was that religion was doing what religion always does, which is adding to the gospel. Those Jewish Christians were taking salvation, which comes through faith in Jesus and what he did on the cross alone, and they were adding to it all these other rules and regulations, like circumcision. They created an equation that looks like this:

Jesus + circumcision = salvation

Now we look at that and think, "Well, that's just silly. You don't have to be circumcised to be a Christian." But the reality is that almost every generation and every culture has been tempted to add something to that equation. For instance:

- Jesus + being immersed in water = salvation
- Jesus + doing Communion a certain way = salvation
- Jesus + voting Republican (or Democrat) = salvation
- Jesus + church membership = salvation

There are dozens and dozens of things that we've tried to force into that blank. And each time we do that, we are mixing law and grace—and becoming dangerously close to making religion into an idol.

Acts 15 is a reminder that religion always tends to complicate what God has made simple. It's always trying to elevate an action or experience to idol status by adding it to Jesus.

> Religion always tends to complicate what God has made simple. It's always trying to elevate an action or experience to idol status by adding it to Jesus.

RELIGIOUS REACTION

But let's look at what happened next. In what appears to be one of the very first church business meetings, the early believers gathered together to discuss the topic of circumcision.

> Then some of the believers who belonged to the party of the Pharisees stood up and said, "The Gentiles must be circumcised and required to keep the law of Moses."
>
> The apostles and elders met to consider this question. After much discussion, Peter got up and addressed them: "Brothers, you know that some time ago God made a choice among you that the Gentiles might hear from my lips the message of the gospel and believe. God, who knows the heart, showed that he accepted them by giving the Holy Spirit to them, just as he did to us. He did not discriminate between us and them, for he purified their hearts by faith." (vv. 5–9)

Did you notice that last verse? It says God made "no distinction" between the two groups. And yet religion always does. Religion not only complicates things; it also divides people.

"Now then, why do you try to test God by putting on the necks of
Gentiles a yoke that neither we nor our ancestors have been able
to bear? No! We believe it is through the grace of our Lord Jesus
that we are saved, just as they are." (vv. 10–11)

The Jews who insisted on circumcision were rebuilding the wall
between Jews and Gentiles that Jesus had torn down on the cross.
They were putting a heavy, unbearable Jewish yoke on the Gentiles'
shoulders. These legalistic Jews were blocking the new and living way
to God that Jesus Christ had opened when he died and rose again.

I remember one of the first doses of this kind of religion that I
ever consumed. It happened when I was in high school. One of my
friends dragged me to a youth revival at a local church. They had set
up a huge tent out in the church parking lot, and we all crowded into
it to see what would happen.

The first thirty minutes or so were filled with sometimes humor-
ous but usually just goofy skits performed by other teens. I didn't
really understand how dressing up in all black and pretending to be a
mime while acting out some contemporary Christian song was supposed to be engaging, but they seemed to be having fun.

When the mimes were done, a preacher stood up and spoke to
all us teenagers. While I can't really remember the details of his message, I certainly remember the main points. They were, basically,
don't smoke, don't cuss, don't drink, don't have sex, and don't play
cards. (I still haven't figured out the cards one.)

The preacher ended the message by begging and pleading in a
very passionate way for those of us who had committed any of the
five abominations to come forward and repent so we could be saved.
I have to admit that at this point of my life I had done four of the five.
I had played cards, I had cussed, and the other two, well, are none of
your business. (This book isn't a tell-all).

But I have to tell you, the way this guy presented this information didn't make me want to confess and start following God. It made me want to go out and do the one thing I hadn't done on the list.

The preacher's focus was not on Jesus and the life he came to offer but on moralism and behavior modification. And I wasn't buying it.

I believe that preacher had fallen for a common ploy of the evil one—to get us on tangents so that we lose sight of what following Jesus is really about. And I see that kind of misdirection so often in youth work. We put too much emphasis on the negative and give our young people the impression that Christianity is a religion of reaction. That's why we lose them as they get older. They see Christianity as a religious straitjacket from which they must escape if they want to have any fun.

The religious-regulation approach to Christianity is all wrong: "Do not handle! Do not taste! Do not touch! Do not try!"

PUT AWAY YOUR PREFERENCES

To return to Acts 15, the discussion about circumcision continued. They debated the issue back and forth, and Paul and Barnabas reported on some of the signs and wonders God had been doing among the Gentiles. Finally James, the brother of Jesus, stood up and gave an amazing speech:

> Brothers . . . listen to me. Simon has described to us how God first intervened to choose a people for his name from the Gentiles. The words of the prophets are in agreement with this, as it is written:
>
> > *"After this I will return*
> > *and rebuild David's fallen tent.*
> > *Its ruins I will rebuild,*
> > *and I will restore it,*

that the rest of mankind may seek the Lord,

even all the Gentiles who bear my name,

says the Lord, who does these things"—

things known from long ago.

It is my judgment, therefore, that we should not make it difficult for the Gentiles who are turning to God." (vv. 13–19)

> This is the tension felt throughout the entire New Testament, the early church, and, I would argue, right up to this very day. What do you do when your religion isn't big enough for God?

Wow. Did you get that? James was striking out hard against religious idolatry, telling his fellow Christians in no uncertain terms not to add to the gospel. Not to put unnecessary hurdles in front of people who are trying to get to God. Not to allow traditions, opinions, or preferences to get in the way of someone who wants to meet and follow Jesus Christ—or in the way of your own discipleship.

The heart of his message: don't trust in those things to give you what only God can give you.

This is serious business, friends. Whenever we add anything to the gospel, we're denying the finished work of Jesus Christ on the cross.

NOT BIG ENOUGH

The big issue in the circumcision controversy was that religion, with all its traditions and preferences, was simply not big enough to contain our God. It was an elaboration of a question that Philip confronted when he met an Ethiopian official on the road to Gaza.

I love the story as it unfolds in Acts 8. It's such a vivid demonstration of the importance of moving past religious idolism to living faith.

What happened, basically, was that Philip was walking down the road and encountered the Ethiopian in his chariot. The fact that the man was reading the book of Isaiah showed that he was interested in Judaism. But the man also happened to be a eunuch, which meant that though he could be a convert to Judaism, he could not fully participate in the worship assembly (Deut. 23:1). Though he was traveling to Jerusalem to worship, he would have still been considered an outsider and foreigner.[1]

As a good, conservative, rule-keeping Jewish follower of Jesus, Philip could have viewed the eunuch as "damaged goods" or as someone who simply didn't qualify to be part of his group. He could have refused to teach him or accept him on that basis. If Philip actually welcomed the foreign eunuch into his faith, he would be violating a tradition he had been raised to respect and follow—and he had also been raised to believe that following traditions determined his standing with God.

This is the tension felt throughout the entire New Testament, the early church, and, I would argue, right up to this very day.

What do you do when your religion isn't big enough for God?

When we make an idol out of religion, we so elevate our group's traditions and preferences that we may severely limit what we believe is possible with God. Maybe God is trying to do something far superior and more compelling than our traditions and preferences have led us to believe is possible.

We all need to begin to understand that God will not play by our rules, be boxed in by our ideas, or dance for the idol of religion.

Fortunately, Philip was able to follow God's leading out of the narrow box of his religion. He took the opportunity first to introduce the Ethiopian eunuch to Jesus and then to baptize him, inviting this foreign outsider into the widening circle of God's welcome. In the process, he found the way out of religious idolatry and into the true freedom of faith.

A trail first blazed by Jesus himself.

LOVE EVERYTHING LESS

I think I get more questions about Jesus' teaching in Luke 14 than probably any other text in the Bible:

> Large crowds were traveling with Jesus, and turning to them he said: "If anyone comes to me and does not hate father and mother, wife and children, brothers and sisters—yes, even their own life—such a person cannot be my disciple." (vv. 25–26)

What? Hate your mother and father? Hate your wife? Your children? What was Jesus talking about?

Well, clearly he's not calling us to actually hate our families. Just a few chapters before this text, when he was asked what the most important law was, he's quoted as saying, "'Love the Lord your God with all your heart and with all your soul and with all your strength and with all your mind'; and, 'Love your neighbor as yourself'" (Luke 10:27).

Later he told his disciples, "This is my command: Love each other" (John 15:17).

So what's going on here?

First, you need to know that Jesus was using hyperbole. He was using exaggeration to make or reinforce a point—something we do all the time.

The other day my son wanted to go to a basketball game, and when I told him we couldn't go, he said, "But Dad, everybody is going to be there." Did he literally mean the world's population of

6.9 billion people would be at that game? No, he was exaggerating to make his point, and I understood exactly what he meant.

I believe Jesus was doing the same thing when he told his followers to hate their families. He was using hyperbole to say, "All other relationships and activities should pale in comparison to following me."

In other words, "Don't take what is good and make it ultimate."

And isn't that what often happens with religion? We take traditions and preferences, which are good and lovely things, and we make them ultimate things. We give them idol status.

After an extended amount of time reflecting on this passage, I once wrote this in my journal: "Pete, your greatest temptation in life will be to chase after not what is ridiculously evil but what is deceptively good."

While I may not know you personally, I believe this is probably your greatest temptation as well.

You see, Jesus never said you can't have religious preferences.

There's nothing wrong with preferring traditional music over contemporary music (or vice versa).

There's nothing wrong with wanting to go to church in a gym or even under a bridge instead of in a building with a steeple.

There's nothing wrong with wanting to take Communion weekly instead of quarterly.

There's nothing wrong with having a heart for social justice, Scripture memory, or being part of a community group.

Jesus just said, don't allow those preferences and traditions to become rules that you force other people to obey if they want to follow him. Don't take good things and make them ultimate things.

Another way to say this is: be careful not to worship a good thing as a god thing, for that is an idolatry thing that will become a destructive thing.

Why? Simply because no religious tradition or preference can

> Your greatest temptation in life will be to chase after not what is ridiculously evil but what is deceptively good.

purify the sinner's heart or give eternal life. No law or rule can ever lead to an explosion of love and joy in the human heart. What the Law could not do, God did through his own Son, Jesus. But religion tends to take the focus off what Christ did and to put it on our own efforts instead. It tends to make us focus on what's in the blank of Jesus + _____ rather than on the cross.

RELIGION VERSUS GOSPEL

I believe this is the major difference between manmade religion, which leads to idolatry, and the God-given gospel, which leads to true transformation.

Martin Luther rightly said that, as sinners, we are prone to pursue a relationship with God through one of two different channels. The first is religion, and the second is the gospel. The two are antithetical in every way.

Religion says that if we obey God, he will love us.

The gospel says that it is because God has loved us through Jesus that we *can* obey.

Religion says that we should trust in what we do as good, moral people.

The gospel says that we should trust in the perfectly sinless life of Jesus because he is the only good and truly moral person who will ever live.

The focus of much religion is to get from God such things as health, wealth, insight, power, and control.

The focus of the gospel is not the gifts God gives but rather God himself—in the form of Jesus—as the gift given to us by grace.

Religion is about what I have to do.

The gospel is about what I get to do.

Religion leads to an uncertainty about my standing before God because I never know if I have done enough to please God.

The gospel leads to a certainty about my standing before God because of the finished work of Jesus on my behalf on the cross.

When we fail to focus on and believe in the truth about who Jesus is, when we miss the impact of his sacrificial death on the cross and triumphal resurrection, we will find it virtually impossible to resist the empty promises of this world—including the promises of religion. Because our lives must be filled by something. That's just the way we're made.

A SEA WITHOUT A SHORE

I'm currently wrapping up a very strenuous season of ministry. Between speaking at my church every week, speaking regularly at church conferences, and just finishing an international book tour, I'm exhausted.

I've got nobody to blame but myself. I've made some poor scheduling decisions that have gotten me here, and I've learned a few tough lessons.

And here's what I'm noticing. When I get tired physically and mentally, I seem to revert to trying to earn God's love.

I allow guilt to overwhelm me.

I allow doubts to sink deep.

I constantly question God's purposes.

I start wondering if he really cares or knows.

This week I was speaking on a cruise ship. (I hope you'll feel sorry for the rough life I live.) It was the first time I had ever been on a ship, much less out in the middle of the sea like that. At one point we spent an entire thirty-six hours at sea without seeing land.

Just imagine the freedom that comes with believing that Jesus truly is enough. What would happen in your life if you began to realize that God doesn't wait or want you to earn his love, but that he, through Jesus, has been pursuing you with love from the very beginning?

It was unreal to stand on the side of that boat and just look out. For hours it was just water and water and water as far as you can see. Just the untamed, fully engulfing, never-ending ocean.

There's a worship song out right now by one of my favorite worship leaders, David Crowder. The song is entitled "Sometimes," and its powerful chorus refers to God's love as "a sea without a shore."[2]

I thought about that beautiful lyric as I read Paul's wonderful words in Romans 8:31–34:

What shall we say about such wonderful things as these? If God is for us, who can ever be against us? Since he did not spare even his own Son but gave him up for us all, won't he also give us everything else? Who dares accuse us whom God has chosen for his own? No one—for God himself has given us right standing with himself. Who then will condemn us? No one—for Christ Jesus died for us and was raised to life for us, and he is sitting in the place of honor at God's right hand, pleading for us. (NLT)

Just think about that. If God is for you, who could be against you? For God himself is pleading for you. The apostle continued:

Can anything ever separate us from Christ's love? Does it mean he no longer loves us if we have trouble or calamity, or are persecuted, or hungry, or destitute, or in danger, or threatened with death? (As the Scriptures say, "For your sake we are killed every day; we are being slaughtered like sheep.") No, despite all these things, overwhelming victory is ours through Christ, who loved us.

And I am convinced that nothing can ever separate us from God's love. Neither death nor life, neither angels nor demons, neither our fears for today nor our worries about tomorrow—not even the powers of hell can separate us from God's love. No power in the sky above or in the earth below—indeed, nothing in all creation will ever be able to separate us from the love of God that is revealed in Christ Jesus our Lord. (vv. 35–39 NLT)

Isn't that an amazing, perspective-changing passage? It hones in on two key reasons religion so easily becomes an idol in our lives:

1. We all have a desperate desire for love.
2. We often think God's love is limited and conditional.

I know that this side of heaven I'll never be able to fully comprehend the enormity of God's love for me and the people of this world, but I'm so thankful for those moments where I get just a little glimpse of his fully engulfing, never-ending love. This love that truly is like a sea without a shore.

And just imagine the freedom that comes with believing that Jesus truly is enough. What would happen in your life if you began to realize that God doesn't wait or want you to earn his love, but that he, through Jesus, has been pursuing you with love from the very beginning?

It's not Jesus plus anything that gives salvation.

It's not Jesus plus anything that offers us purpose, comfort, or security.

It's not Jesus plus anything that defines our identity.

It's just Jesus. Anything else is just an empty promise.

CHAPTER EIGHT
ADDICTED TO BEAUTY

As a young girl of fourteen, Annie spent her afternoons flipping through old photo albums, staring at pictures of her mother at the same age. But this was not just a harmless activity. It was an expression of pain.

Annie is a friend of mine. I've known her for years, and I've always been aware that image was extremely important to her. She is one of those women who always looks perfectly put together—every hair in place, makeup just right, all the right clothes. For as long as I have known her it has been obvious to me that her sense of identity and worth was deeply steeped in making sure she looked attractive in the eyes of other people. But I never had a clue where this excessive concern with appearance came from until the day she told me it was rooted in the way her mother had treated her.

"How so?" I asked. "How does your mom play into this?" She went on to tell me one of the most twisted and heartbreaking stories I've ever heard.

"When I was fourteen years old, I was really starting to notice that certain girls got attention for looking a particular way, while other girls were often ignored or looked down upon. Of course, I wanted to be thought of as pretty, so I did everything I could to imitate the girls I thought were viewed that way. From what I wore to the makeup that I put on to how I styled my hair, it became what I constantly thought about.

"I spent hours flipping through my mom's pictures from when she was a teenager. She was so beautiful. I wondered if I would ever be as pretty as she was.

"One night I was getting ready to go out and meet some friends at the mall. As I got into the car with my mom, she looked at me and said, 'What in the world are you doing?'

"I said, 'What, Mom?'

"She said, 'Annie, you can't go out tonight without makeup on. Are you crazy? You look horrible.'

"As a fourteen-year-old girl, my mom's comments had an unmistakable impact on me. A year later, I would be grounded to my room for a week for not wearing makeup to school one day. And the night of my high school prom, she walked into my room just minutes before my date was to arrive. In a fit of rage she reached out and messed up my carefully arranged hair, screaming, 'You can't go out like this! Your hair looks horrible! Now fix it right!'"

As Annie told me her story that afternoon, I noticed her hands were shaking. And as I thought about all the verbal and psychological abuse she had endured, so much about her behavior made sense. I now understood why she had made an idol out of beauty—depending on her appearance to give her the affirmation that only God could give her.

THE PUNISHING LOOP

My friend Annie is not alone—far from it. According to a recent survey, on average, women have thirteen negative body thoughts daily[1]—thoughts like:

- *I'm too fat.*
- *I'm too thin.*
- *My breasts are too small.*
- *My ears are too big.*
- *My hair is too curly.*
- *I'm worthless.*
- *No man will ever want me.*

Such self-criticism starts early. Another study showed that nearly half of all three- to six-year-old girls were already worried about being fat, and roughly one-third of them said they wanted to change something about their bodies.[2]

And appearance issues are certainly not limited to women and girls. Men struggle with this as well. I still remember at a very early age being concerned with having the latest and greatest tennis shoes. I remember kids in seventh grade making fun of a jacket I wore to school. I remember being mortified when I started getting acne.

Most of us discover very early in life that the way we look seems to carry a lot of weight in our culture.

Pick up any magazine.

Watch any commercial.

Walk into any room and see where the eyes of the crowd are focused.

Being beautiful really can help me get what I want—for a while. It's hard to argue with the fact that good-looking people are often rewarded with jobs, friendships, relationships, and attention. But appearance, just like all the other idols we've looked at, eventually shows itself as an empty promise.

Television, movies, magazines, and advertisements bombard us daily with the same empty promises:

- "How to be beautiful in ten days or less."
- "How to look twenty years younger."
- "Lose that ugly cellulite."
- "Shampoo with this and you'll combat that baldness."
- "Use this product and women will flock to you."

And all for what? The perfect body. The polished image. The right look.

But it's more than just that, isn't it? This is about fulfillment. This is about wanting to feel admired, desired, and ultimately, loved. In a sense it's another power issue—controlling how others respond to us. And our dominant culture seems fully invested in worshipping the idol of appearance.

Several years back, British artist Marc Quinn made the news for creating a life-size gold sculpture of supermodel Kate Moss that is reportedly worth nearly three million dollars. When asked about why he created the largest such creation built since ancient Egypt, Quinn said, "I thought the next thing to do would be to make a sculpture of the person who's the ideal beauty of the moment."[3]

This sculpture is evidence of how society celebrates super models as examples of physical perfection—an over-the-top example of our tendency to worship at the altar of beauty.

Now, take just a second to reflect on whether or not this might be something you struggle with.

- Do you have a hard time concentrating if you don't feel you look your best?
- Are you easily annoyed by, envious of, or judgmental of those who represent a kind of beauty you think you could never attain? For instance, do you tend to make snarky remarks about the young, the blond, the buff, or the impossibly thin?

- Do you tend to be more concerned about how you look on the outside than who you're becoming on the inside?
- Do you tend to make snap judgments about people when you first see them?
- Do you occasionally have moments when you realize you're spending an inappropriate amount on hair, makeup, gym memberships, clothing, or other appearance-related items? Have you ever vowed to cut back and then couldn't do it?
- Do you spend more time reading about how to look more attractive than you do allowing your soul to be shaped by God's Word?
- Do you regularly replay negative things people have said about your appearance, to the point of it often affecting your mood?
- Do you care more about looking like you just walked out of a magazine than you do about becoming the man or woman God created you to be?

I would be surprised if at least one or two of these didn't hit home. The truth is, in this culture it's hard to escape worshipping at the altar of appearance. So let's look at some of the foundational lies our culture has fed us about how we look.

LIE #1: BEING BEAUTIFUL WILL GET ME WHAT I WANT

Actually, in the short term, this first statement isn't a lie at all. But the important phrase here is *in the short term.*

Being beautiful really can help me get what I want—for a while. It's hard to argue with the fact that good-looking people are often rewarded with jobs, friendships, relationships, and attention. But appearance, just like all the other idols we've looked at, eventually shows itself as an empty promise.

There are several reasons for this. For one thing, beauty itself eventually fades. It's a built-in process as we age. And while diet and exercise and hair coloring and plastic surgery can delay the process, they cannot stop it. For purely physical reasons, the idol of appearance eventually lets everyone down.

But even if looks could be maintained forever, appearance would be an empty promise because it cannot deliver what we ask of it. External beauty cannot bring us the internal satisfaction we hope so desperately that it will.

Never Enough

The story of Rachel in the Bible (Gen. 29–30) is a great example of this. We looked at this story earlier from the point of view of Rachel's eventual husband, Jacob. But let's look at it again from Rachel's point of view.

Rachel, remember, had been supremely blessed in the looks department. She was far more beautiful than her older sister, Leah. In fact, she was so gorgeous that when Jacob first laid eyes on her, he instantly fell in love with her. He even agreed to work for her father, Laban, a total of fourteen years to win her hand in marriage. Fourteen years! When Laban tricked him into marrying Leah first, he persisted until he won Rachel too. That's how much she meant to him.

Rachel was beautiful, and she had her husband's love and devotion. No woman could want for more, right?

Wrong.

The more that Rachel wanted was basically what we all want: what we don't have. And what Rachel didn't have was children.

Rachel's jealousy and frustration escalated as she watched Leah give birth to six sons in a row, then a daughter. Every time one of those babies cried, each time one of those chidren had a birthday— every milestone must have been a painful reminder to Rachel that her life wasn't where she wanted it to be. Despite being so blessed, she couldn't focus on anything but what she didn't have.

In a moment of total desperation she finally screamed at Jacob, "Give me children, or I'll die!" (Gen. 30:1). She was basically declaring that her life was not worth living unless she had children.

Though Rachel had beauty, she longed desperately for a child to prove her worth and significance. But what would happen once she got a child?

We don't have to wonder because Genesis lays the whole thing out for us. God was gracious to Rachel, and she finally had a son of her own. She named him Joseph, which means "Let me add another."

See what was happening here? Even in the moment where Rachel finally got what she thought she wanted, she realized it was an empty promise and longed for something else—in this case, another child. It was something she believed she had to have, and so she made it her god.

> This is the very nature of idolatry and empty promises. Whenever what you're pursuing to give you what only God can give you fails, you move on to the next thing.

This is the very nature of idolatry and empty promises. Whenever what you're pursuing to give you what only God can give you fails, you move on to the next thing.

Now, wanting children was not what made Rachel idolatrous. There's nothing wrong with wanting to have children, just as there's nothing inherently wrong with wanting to look good. No, Rachel was idolatrous because her desire for children was her foremost desire. It's what she had to have in order to feel complete and alive.

And the great irony is that the more we focus on an idol, the less fulfilled we feel on the inside. Our lifelong search ends in emptiness, never attaining the satisfaction we crave, because the idols we depend on—especially appearance—are not capable of fulfilling their promises.

Gotta Have It

I'm embarrassed at how many times I've fallen into this same trap as Rachel and screamed (out loud or inwardly), "Give me this, or I think I'm going to die."

Is there anything in your life these days that your heart so longs for that you think, *I must have that for my life to be happy and meaningful?*

If you answer that question with anything other than God, then you know that's your idol. That's what functions as your god.

- *If I were just a little better looking, then I would be happy.*
- *If I could just get married, then I would feel complete.*
- *If we could just have a child, then I would be fulfilled.*
- *If we just lived in a bigger house, then I would be satisfied.*
- *If I could just make vice president (or CEO), that would do it for me.*

Sound familiar? If so, you might have already discovered the catch—which is that anything other than God will eventually disappoint you. Focusing on appearance or anything that this world puts importance on will leave you miserable, sad, and hopeless because it can't heal your inner emptiness.

The Destructive Trap

I believe that most of the time we have no clue just how deadly idols like appearance can actually be. We have no idea the destructive roads these empty promises can lead us down.

Jesus was very clear about this when he said, "The thief's purpose is to steal and kill and destroy" (John 10:10 NLT). There is no faster, more effective way for the thief to lead us into destruction than to get us to buy into one of his empty promises. And I absolutely believe that one of the most widespread plans the evil one has set for our culture is this empty promise that comes along with elevating this elusive trait we call beauty.

Think about just how widespread it is. Every year Americans spend some 20 billion dollars on cosmetics, 2 billion on hair products, 74 billion on diet foods, and 7.4 million on cosmetic surgery.[4] Huge numbers of young men and women are falling into the destructive trap of placing all their hopes on how they look. And many are reaping the consequences not only in disappointment but actual physical and psychological danger.

Take my friend Michelle Myers, for instance. Michelle told me the first time she thought she was fat was when she was eight years old. She vividly recalls sitting between two of her friends at a school assembly. She told me, "It wasn't so much the size of my legs that got to me. It was that I noticed my legs were bigger than both of my friends' legs. I quickly sat back in my chair, holding my legs just above the seat so my legs wouldn't 'smash out.' I literally never let my legs rest on a chair the rest of elementary school unless they were totally hidden underneath my desk."

Michelle struggled with body image the rest of her growing-up years. During her freshman year of college, she contracted mononucleosis, which not only made her feel tired but also killed her appetite. For six weeks she ate barely enough to get by. When she went back to the doctor's office, she knew she had lost weight. But she had no idea how much she'd lost until she stood on the scale. "I remember the nurse gasped as she adjusted the weighted tabs on the scale. The nurse said, 'Girl, when you were here six weeks ago, you weighed 138 pounds. Today, you're only 118.'"

This new reality turned out to be a dark moment for Michelle as her lifelong battle with this particular idol took a dangerous turn. She had entered the frightening new world of anorexia nervosa.

Michelle did the math in her head there in the doctor's office. She thought, *If I lost 3.5 pounds a week without working out, how much weight could I lose if I added working out back into my schedule?*

Michelle made a vow that day that she would do whatever it took to get down to "the perfect weight"—which was far less than her present weight of 118. This new goal consumed her life. She exercised for hours each day and held herself to a very legalistic diet of just sixteen hundred calories a day. Another six weeks later, she was down to 105 pounds.

She recalled, "I couldn't go anywhere without getting compliments. Ladies at church wanted to know my secret. Girls I didn't even know would give me jealous stares when they passed me in public. More surprising than any of these new conversations, though, was that I started getting a lot of attention from guys at college. As a girl who had always been 'one of the guys,' this was new territory for me, and I loved the attention.

"It may be hard for people to believe," she added, "but while weighing just over 100 pounds, I still felt fat. So my meals got smaller and smaller, and then I started skipping meals and taking multiple appetite suppressants and fat burners."

With all the new attention Michelle was getting, she decided to start competing in local beauty pageants. While backstage at the Miss Tennessee pageant, all the girls were fussing over how thin she was. She remembers, "I was half-listening to their complaints about how small I was. But I was more preoccupied with how I looked in the mirror. I couldn't stop looking in the mirror and wishing my tummy would just be a little smaller."

One of the other contestants challenged her to step up on the scale to see just how much she weighed. Still thinking she weighed around 100, she stepped on the scale to discover that she weighed only 89 pounds.

About that point, Michelle started to realize she had a real problem, but she didn't know what to do. To complicate matters, the solid relationship she had with God was starting to dissolve.

As we've seen throughout this book, it's impossible to worship the empty promises of this world and still make God your number one priority. Remember what Jesus said about money? "No one can serve two masters. Either you will hate the one and love the other, or you will be devoted to the one and despise the other" (Matt. 6:24). It applies to other idols too, including beauty.

In Michelle's case, it was guilt that pushed her further and further away from faith. She told me, "How could God possibly use the girl who held Communion in her mouth without swallowing? I would wait until the prayer, sneak out of the aisle to the bathroom, and spit the bread and grape juice into the toilet. I couldn't even bring myself to sacrifice ten calories to remember the fact that he suffered a horrible death and sacrificed himself so I could spend eternity with him."

> It's impossible to worship the empty promises of this world and still make God your number one priority.

But on April 14, 2005, God finally got Michelle's full attention. After thirteen days without a single meal, she went for a run as part of her training for a full marathon. But at mile nineteen her vision started to blur. She tripped and came crashing to the ground. All 84 pounds hit the pavement and, as she remembers, "I literally felt like every brittle bone in my body cracked simultaneously."

Michelle doesn't remember how long she blacked out. But eventually she became conscious again and limped back to the car, realizing she was in desperate need of help. That day she finally admitted to friends and family members—and to God—that something was seriously wrong with her. And in that moment she began the long and slow road to recovery.

Michelle is just one of approximately seven million women and girls and another million men and boys who struggle with eating disorders. Her story is being played out every day around the world in the lives of millions of people. And while these complex disorders probably involve more than simply an obsession with appearance—genetic factors, psychological profile, personal history, even mineral deficiencies may play a role[5]—our cultural emphasis on thinness is clearly implicated.

Eating disorders aren't the only potentially destructive consequences of our national obsession with appearance. Without a doubt, worshipping at the altar of appearance can have dangerous results, and the stakes seem to be rising.

Just last week I read about a San Francisco mother who had been injecting her eight-year-old daughter with Botox to minimize her "wrinkles."

Yes, you read it right—eight years old. And why? In the cutthroat world of children's beauty pageants, the Botox apparently gives her a competitive edge. The mom's defense was "everyone's doing it." Apparently it's a pageant secret used by many pageant moms.[6] But who knows what the fallout will be as more and more people grow up in a society that is willing to sacrifice anything—even health and well-being—on the altar of appearance.

LIE #2: HOW I LOOK IS WHO I AM

John is a successful businessman here in Nashville. He's someone I admire for a myriad of reasons, including his family life. When we get together, I love to pepper him with questions about parenting, business, and life in general.

At a recent lunch I asked John how things were going with his wife, Kim, and their grown daughters.

"I'm glad you asked," he said. "We just had a major breakthrough in our family."

He continued, "Last week all the girls and their families were over to the house for dinner. We were all sitting around just laughing and catching up with each other. For the most part the conversation was dominated with small talk about the weather, our jobs, and the grandkids' latest accomplishments. Then I was showing the kids our latest iPhone app. Kim and I have been using it since January to count our calories. The two of us have collectively lost twenty-one pounds in the past four months just by counting our calories.

"Then the strangest thing happened, Pete. As I was showing all the girls this new app, my oldest daughter, Leslie, started to cry uncontrollably. We all just sat there staring at her, wondering what in the world was going on or what had been said that would set this off. Her mother, who was sitting right next to her, put an arm around her and asked, 'Leslie, what's wrong, sweetie?'

"She started to pull herself together and said, 'Dad, I need to share something with you that has bothered me for years.' Looking me right in the eyes, she said, 'Dad, one day when I was twelve years old, you told me that I was looking a little chubby. Your remark has haunted me for the past twenty-two years. Hardly a day has gone by, and certainly never a week, that I don't think about those words you spoke to me. I know you weren't trying to hurt me, but it's had a huge negative impact on my life.'"

Stunned by John's story, I asked him, "What did you say?"

He answered, "I started to cry with her and told her I was so sorry. When she was a little girl, there were times she leaned toward being slightly overweight. I wanted to protect her. I wanted to help her make healthy choices. I never imagined in a million years my careless words would have such an impact on her. Thank God she was brave enough to be honest with me so we can start working on healing that broken part of our relationship."

As a pastor it would be really tempting for me to preach a minisermon here about how our words, every one of them, have a tremendous impact and influence on the people around us and shape their lives. But what I want to focus on is the fact that John's daughter Leslie had allowed the negative comment her dad made about her appearance to become a part of who she thought she was. Because she thought of herself as chubby, she often pictured herself as being unwanted and rejected.

Like so many in our culture today, she had been shaped by the idolatrous lie that says, "How I look is who I am."

My friend Michelle, whose anorexia also fed off this lie, just wrote an amazing little book called *The Look That Kills*, which recounts her story and her recovery in hopes of helping other young women caught in this vicious addiction. She wrote,

> Even as a child and throughout adolescence, my friends and I dreamed of being Miss America, an actress, or a supermodel— anything that would verify our beauty. It doesn't end with adolescence. In the United States alone, women spend more money annually on beauty products than our nation spends on education. Women—God fearing women included—put too much focus on external beauty.[7]

Michelle has finally gotten to a point where she realizes that who she is and how she looks are not the same thing at all. These days she seeks to please God with her heart more than she seeks to please the world with her appearance. She continued,

> To me, being beautiful in God's eyes involves knowing His word, keeping His commands, and humility. When I think of these traits, I can't help but see smiles, joy, and laughter. A woman possessing a personality like this cannot help but radiate on the outside. Her heart is so full of God that it cannot help but manifest

itself on the outside. We should live our lives in such a way that in order to grasp the depths of our beauty, one must first understand the magnificence of the God we serve.[8]

REAL BEAUTY

Oh, if we could only rest in the truth that we are uniquely created by our heavenly Father (Ps. 139:14). That the God of this universe designed us, loves us, and fully approves of us—including the way we look. I believe the beginning of a healthy self-image is seeing our-selves as God sees us—no more and no less. In him and him alone will we find the approval and validation our hearts long for.

The desire to look attractive is not wrong in and of itself. It's the place of prominence it occupies in your heart that can make it an idol and therefore supremely destruc-tive. Striving to find significance, acceptance, or power based on the beauty standards of this world will leave you empty, hurt, and ultimately destroyed.

> There are few things more attractive than seeing someone who is whole—whole as only a person who is fully submitted to God can be.

I love the imagery Isaiah gave us of God as the potter and each one of us being the clay. He said,

> Yet you, Lord, are our Father.
> We are the clay, you are the potter;
> we are all the work of your hand. (Isa. 64:8)

Only a submitted life can be shaped and molded by the Potter. When we finally give up our own ambitions for a beauty that will win the love of others, he is then free to make the heap of once-useless clay into a beautiful piece of art.

There are few things more attractive than seeing someone who is whole—whole as only a person who is fully submitted to God can be. Someone who accepts herself as God created and continues to shape her to be. That's a person of real beauty—the kind that truly lasts and satisfies.

I want to close this chapter with what I believe to be a moving piece from Margery William's children's classic, *The Velveteen Rabbit.* This conversation between a little stuffed rabbit and an older, wiser nursery toy sums up what I believe to be true beauty:

"What is REAL?" asked the Rabbit one day, when they were lying side by side near the nursery fender, before Nana came to tidy the room. "Does it mean having things that buzz inside you and a stick-out handle?"

"Real isn't how you are made," said the Skin Horse. "It's a thing that happens to you. When a child loves you for a long, long time, not just to play with, but REALLY loves you, then you become Real."

"Does it hurt?" asked the Rabbit.

"Sometimes," said the Skin Horse, for he was always truthful. "When you are Real you don't mind being hurt."

"Does it happen all at once, like being wound up," he asked, "or bit by bit?"

"It doesn't happen all at once," said the Skin Horse. "You become. It takes a long time. That's why it doesn't often happen to people who break easily, or have sharp edges, or who have to be carefully kept. Generally, by the time you are Real, most of your hair has been loved off, and your eyes drop out and you get loose in the joints and very shabby. But these things don't matter at all, because once you are Real you can't be ugly, except to people who don't understand."[9]

CHAPTER NINE
CHASING A DREAM

I believe most people have a pretty clear picture in their minds of what they want their futures to look like. In fact, I think many of these dreams begin in our hearts from a fairly early age.

The stereotypical American dream includes a big house, a worthwhile (and lucrative) career, and a good marriage to an attractive spouse so you can have smart, beautiful children who look good for the yearly Christmas card photo and newsletter. Your dream may be a little different, but I bet it includes some variation of what I just described. And while you may not have ever written this dream down somewhere, it's likely deeply etched in your mind. You probably have dreams about

- where you want to be in your career or vocation;
- where you'd like to live;
- what your marriage will be like;
- what your kids will accomplish;
- the kind of mark you'll make on the world.

Some of these dreams might be so desirable that you begin to think they can give you what only God can give. You may even be tempted to abandon your God-given values in the pursuit of your God-given dreams.

But your dreams, no matter how wonderful they may be, will always make a lousy god.

We spend so much of our lives trying to control and manipulate events in a desperate attempt to cling tightly to the pictures of our futures. Yet, over and over again throughout Scripture we see God asking people to willingly and even joyfully release the death grip on the pictures of their futures and trust God with how their lives turn out.

> Your dreams, no matter how wonderful they may be, will always make a lousy god.

One such person was Abraham in the Old Testament.

I identify with Abraham because he seems like such an average Joe. Nothing too spectacular is ever really mentioned of him. No special gifts. He is not a charismatic leader and has no huge accomplishments that I'm aware of.

He's just an everyday guy like you and me.

I assume that he had dreams for his life as most of us do. It's important to realize this, because when we think about biblical characters like Abraham, we tend to think that they're just sitting around waiting for God to show up and speak to them. But Abraham, like you, was probably working on his own picture of his future when God first approached him.

Think about it. The man had an established life. He had a wife and an extended family. He had made a name for himself in his community—in those days he was known as Abram—and had accrued material wealth. He was probably thinking about how to provide for his retirement while taking care of his household. He was probably managing a number of different tasks and issues that had bombarded his life. And I imagine there were more than a few restless nights when Abram wondered about where his life was going—if he would be able to keep track of all that was involved in this picture of the future he held in his mind and his heart.

Perhaps it was during one of those sleepless nights that God interrupted Abram's life with these incredible words:

> Go from your country, your people and your father's household to
> the land I will show you.

> *I will make you into a great nation,*
> *and I will bless you;*
> *I will make your name great,*
> *and you will be a blessing.*
> *I will bless those who bless you,*
> *and whoever curses you I will curse;*
> *and all peoples on earth*
> *will be blessed through you. (Gen. 12:1–3)*

WAIT AND SEE

If there is anything that can drive kids into a peak of frustration, it's hearing their parents say the dreaded words, "Wait and see."

"Dad, can we play video games later?"

"We'll wait and see."

"Dad, is it going to snow?"

"Wait and see."

"Dad, can we go sledding?"

"Wait and see."

"Dad, where are we going to eat tonight?"

"Wait and see."

"Dad, can we go to Toys 'R' Us on Saturday?"

"No."

Kids want to know right now. "Are we doing this? I need to know." And the reality is even as adults we don't like the ambiguity. We don't like the unknown. We want to know what's going to happen and when it's going to happen and what we need to do to make sure it happens faster.

But that's not what God gave Abram. Instead, he just told him to "go . . . to the land I will show you."

Can't you imagine how that conversation must have gone?

God says, "Go."

Abram says, "Where?"

"To the land I will show you."

"Where is that?"

"You'll have to wait and see."

"Wait and see? *Wait and see?* This is my life here! Wait and see?"

Ever been forced to leave what is familiar? Ever been in a place in your life where you didn't know where you were going? Maybe you prayed,

- "God, when is my marriage going to get easier?"
- "God, when will I be able to go to bed at night and not worry about money?"
- "God, when are we going to have a baby?"
- "God, when will I meet someone who will hold me, love me, share life with me?"
- "God, will I ever be healthy again?"

And maybe the only answer you got was "Wait and see." If so, you probably have some idea how Abram felt.

But despite the vagueness of God's orders, Abram obeyed. Genesis 12 tells us,

So Abram went, as the LORD had told him; and Lot went with him. Abram was seventy-five years old when he set out from Harran. He took his wife Sarai, his nephew Lot, all the possessions they had accumulated and the people they had acquired in Harran, and they set out for the land of Canaan, and they arrived there. (vv. 4–5)

Now, since Abram did what God told him to do, it was time for the reward, right? After all, God had made a promise. Abram must have assumed that once he had done what God told him, his dreams would start coming true. Sarai would start having children and those children would have children, and Abram's family would grow into a great nation. I'm sure Abram couldn't wait. I assume he was thinking, *It's time for my name to be great. It's time for me to be blessed.*

Isn't that the way most of us think it works? God calls. We listen. We obey. God blesses. Presto. The blessings come flowing down from heaven.

Maybe you have a dream God has placed in your heart, and you're convinced that God has called you to do something about it. You're convinced that you've listened and obeyed. And now you're expecting God to do his part and bless your plans.

But look what happened next to Abram after he obeyed God: "Now there was a famine in the land, and Abram went down to Egypt to live there for a while because the famine was severe" (v. 10).

In other words, God called. Abram listened and obeyed. But God didn't bless—at least not right away. In fact, the very next thing that happened to Abram was a calamity—a severe famine that forced him to move yet again.

I've discovered that most of us have a tendency to reduce God to what is safe and predictable and accords with our sense of what is fair and just and right. We are continually tempted to formulate equations that predict what God will do: if you do this, then God will always do that.

However, a central theme throughout the Bible is that while God is indeed just, he is anything but safe and predictable. He is God. We're not. And he simply cannot be reduced to an equation that we then worship.

> While God is indeed just, he is anything but safe and predictable. He is God. We're not. And he simply cannot be reduced to an equation that we then worship.

Sometimes we'll step out in faith and immediately see results. That's what happened after God told Joshua and his priests to step into the Jordan River. They stepped, and the waters receded (Joshua 3).

But that's not always how God works. I'd even say that's not *usually* the way God works. This journey of faith with God looks different in everyone's life. Why? Because God cares more about who we're becoming than where we're going.

Yes, God keeps his promises. But one thing God never promises is that following him will be easy, smooth, or painless.

Abram wandered for many years. He faced difficulties of all kinds as he waited for his God-given dream to come true. I imagine there were times he wanted to scream at the top of his lungs, "God, I gave up everything for you! I've risked all I held so safe and secure in my hands, and now what do I have?"

All he got in reply was more promises—more "wait and see." Again and again, Abram was left to choose.

Either he trusted God with his future, or he didn't.

I believe we all face situations in life where we have to choose whether or not to trust God enough to relinquish the death grip we have on the pictures we've created for our futures. Because like it or not, it's quite possible that our pictures may be full of potential idols vying for our worship and attention.

ARE WE THERE YET?

I don't know about you, but I love road trips. I always have. I love packing for road trips. I love laying all my snacks out. I love loading my iPod and making a soundtrack for the trip.

With three boys, however, my road trips have changed a bit. I still thoroughly enjoy them, but they're a little more complicated and stressful. And there is one little question my boys ask over and over that comes dangerously close to robbing me of the joy of a good road trip.

I bet you can guess the question:

"Dad, are we there yet?"

We can be on our way to visit family in Toledo, Ohio—about a five-hundred-mile journey. And by the time we're on the far edge of Nashville, one of my boys will inevitably ask, "Dad, are we there yet?"

There are times I want to respond with, "Of course we're not there yet, son. Do you notice the car is still moving? When the car stops and I announce we're there, then we're there."

But I know better. I know my kids aren't really asking a question as much as they're making a statement. When they ask, "Are we there yet?" what they're really saying is, "We're tired, we're bored, and we want out."

In Genesis 15:1 we read:

After this, the word of the Lord came to Abram in a vision:

> *"Do not be afraid, Abram.*
> *I am your shield,*
> *your very great reward."*

Did you notice that first phrase, "After this"? You automatically have to ask, "After what?"

And the answer is "ten years." God was coming to Abram after a full decade of unfulfilled promise.

Ten years of tears.

Ten years of wondering if the dream would ever come true.

Ten years of "Are we there yet?"

After all this, God said to Abram, "I am your shield, your very great reward."

God was saying, *"I'm* your reward. I'm going to give you *me.* Abram, don't worship my gifts. Don't think for a second that the things I bless you with are the real gifts. I'm the real gift. I'm the real reward."

But Abram wasn't buying it. Look at the next verses:

> But Abram said, "Sovereign LORD, what can you give me since I
> remain childless and the one who will inherit my estate is Eliezer
> of Damascus?" And Abram said, "You have given me no children;
> so a servant in my household will be my heir." (vv. 2–3)

Can't you sense the frustration? Abram was basically saying, "Great. I'm so glad you're with me, but you promised I was going to be the father of a great nation, and I don't even have a son yet."

How many God-given dreams do you have that are still unfulfilled?

- A dream to see your grown children settled down and happy?
- A dream for healing from a particular illness?
- A dream to go to college or graduate school?
- A dream to build a business or write a book?

A few years ago Brandi and I spent time ministering to a young single woman. We had her over for dinner a couple of nights a week and got to know her pretty well. Melody was a lovely young woman, but she was totally obsessed with getting married. It was all she dreamed of, all she talked about. And the longer that dream went unfulfilled, the more frustrated she became.

Every one of our conversations over dinner was a variation of "Are we there yet?"

When Melody finally met a likely prospect, she was overjoyed. Despite warnings from several of her friends that she was rushing into marriage, she proceeded full steam ahead. But within weeks of the wedding, we saw disappointment on Melody's face. It was obvious her dream wasn't living up to what she thought it would be.

So what was next? Melody became obsessed with having a child. She and her husband started trying right after the honeymoon, and with every month that went by that she wasn't pregnant her unhappiness grew more intense.

More "Are we there yet?"

When I look at Melody's life now, I can see it has been a series of bitter disappointments for her. She continues to this day to be obsessed with the next thing she thinks will bring her value or significance or worth. For some reason she's blinded to the raving idolatry in her life, her insistence on trusting in her dreams instead of in God.

Last I heard she was dreaming about finding a new house because the one she and her husband live in now just isn't what she wants.

Melody's an extreme case, but I think many of us have experienced the "Are we there yet?" mentality to one degree or another. We *know* we're not there, but we want God to know we're tired of waiting, weary of wondering if it's ever going to happen.

If you're currently living with such an unfulfilled dream, more than likely you understand where Abram was coming from. Maybe, like him, you've got an attitude with God. You've heard all the promises, all the clichés, all the points, and now you want something to change. You may even become consumed by the need to salvage what you've left behind instead of continuing to move forward.

But God's word to Abram—and to any of us who are getting impatient about our unfulfilled dreams—was this:

You're missing the point.

The prize is me.

I'm your reward.

I can give you what none of these earthly blessings can or will ever give you.

Now if you know the story of Abram, you know that God did eventually fulfill his promises. Not only did he give him a new name—Abraham—but he also granted him a miracle son in his old age. With the arrival of Isaac, Abraham's long-awaited dream finally came true. His patience and his obedience had their reward.

But Abraham's story wasn't over.

In fact, Abraham was about to learn a very difficult lesson. A lesson we can never forget:

God loves you enough to strip you of anything that keeps you from him—even if it's your most cherished dream.

> I've often thought it was quite ironic that I have actually trusted God for my salvation and my eternity, yet I struggle so much to trust him with the small details of my picture.

Abraham eventually followed God into one of the most nerve-racking moments of his life—when God asked him to give up his only son, Isaac. He was challenged to sacrifice the one thing in this world that was most precious to him. And Abraham obeyed, laying both his family and his future on the line.

Yes, this story had a happy ending. God provided a substitute sacrifice at the last minute, and Isaac grew up to father the next generation of the great nation God had promised. But when Abraham chose to trust God, he had no idea the situation would turn out that way. He had just learned, through long years of following, to put his faith in his Father, not in his future. He chose to believe, and as James 2:23 says, that belief "was credited to him as righteousness."

DEFINED BY A PROMISE

The sin of unbelief lies at the heart of all other sins and particularly at the heart of idolatry. As Dallas Willard explained,

> Ideas and images are the primary focus of Satan's efforts to defeat God's purposes for humankind. They form the primary arena of the battle of spiritual formation. When we are subject to Satan's chosen ideas and images, he can take a holiday. When he undertook to draw eve away from God, he did not hit her with a stick, but with an idea. It was with the idea that God could not be trusted and that she must act on her own to secure her own well-being.[1]

Eve was deceived into thinking that God was holding out on her and that happiness and fulfillment could be found outside of what God had said. The lives of so many of us have gone wrong at the exact same place as Eve's. We've allowed the seduction of an empty promise to whisper into our hearts. We've begun to think that the apple, the dream, could somehow give us something that God could not give us, that somehow God has been holding out on us.

Every time I worship something or someone other than God, I'm forgetting that he's a good God and great Father who can be trusted. Though he's proven his faithfulness to me over and over, I still fall back into the habits of idolatry. I've often thought it was quite ironic that I have actually trusted God for my salvation and my eternity, yet I struggle so much to trust him with the small details of my picture.

So when I read about someone like Abraham, who trusted God radically with what mattered most to him, I have to ask how. How did he do it? Why did he do it?

I believe Abraham's faith was built on some words God gave him in the original promise. In the midst of a life filled with uncertainty, and with a call on his life that was going to bring more uncertainty, God gave Abraham two words to live by:

I will. I . . . will.

In fact, six times in God's original conversation with Abraham (Gen. 12), God said, in some way or another, "I will." He said it six times in the first three verses of Abraham's story.

Just think about all the things God could have said, but didn't:

God didn't say, "I might."

God didn't say, "I'll try my best."

God didn't say, "I'll think about it."

God didn't say, "You will."

God defined himself by a promise: "I will."

I realize you may be facing heavy discouragement or deep heartache because you hold tightly in your hands a very detailed picture of the way you hoped your life would turn out. When you compare that picture with reality, the differences are obvious.

But I firmly believe that if you are willing to trust the God who says, "I will," nothing that is of eternal value in this life is at risk. You ultimately have nothing to fear.

Fear enters our minds and begins to take over when we cling too tightly to those pictures of what we think our futures should look like, elevating them to idolatry status and diminishing the Artist of those very pictures.

It's those unexpected shattered-dream moments that provide us with twists and turns in life where we meet God. Rarely do we surrender when we feel strong and in control. But when a dream is shattered, when life takes an unexpected turn and veers out of control, that's when we fall to our knees. That's when a new dream can grow.

There's a lot about what happens to us in life that we cannot control. What we can control, however, is our willingness to seek God in the midst of all the craziness. Surrendering doesn't mean we spend less energy on pursuing our dreams, but it does mean we spend less nervous energy. It means we see our dreams for what they are—possibilities and promises and goals, not sources of our peace and security. It means our confidence is no longer in our ability to achieve each one of our dreams, but in the strength and power of the God we claim to follow.

How do you get there? All it takes is a moment where, like Abraham, you relinquish your grip on your picture of your future and say, "Jesus, I want to trust you with that. Even if it means risking all the stuff I think is valuable, all the good things I'm waiting for, I'm still going to trust you."

And maybe even in this moment, God is showing you something in your life that you know you need to let go of—or at least hold with open hands. It may be something good. It may even be something from him. But it's something you've been trusting to give you what only God can provide.

Often we're unaware that we even have an idol until our dreams get threatened. This is a fundamental truth about idolatry: prosperity tends to mask our idols; crisis tends to reveal them.

As long as things are going well in my life, as long as my picture of the way I want life to turn out matches up with the picture of my reality, I don't think I have an idol problem. But when there is a crisis, then all of a sudden I realize, "Man, I've been banking on this dream in a way that no dream should be banked on."

Our dreams, no matter how great or noble they may be, always make lousy gods.

CHAPTER TEN
YOU ARE WHAT YOU WORSHIP

The guy came out of nowhere, pulling out right in front of me as I drove down the street. I slammed on my brakes and came to a screeching stop. My four-year-old, Brewer, took me by surprise too. Without hesitation he leaned forward in his car seat and yelled, "You idiot!"

"Son, we don't talk like that," I reprimanded, fighting back a grin and thinking, *I've got to ask Brandi where he's learning this stuff.*

Then, a day or two later, a guy tried to cut over into my lane of traffic while I was on the way to work. Under my breath I muttered, "What are you doing, you idiot?" Then the lightbulb came on. That's where Brewer had heard that word. He had heard me say it to other drivers. He doesn't even know what the word *idiot* means, but he'd learned from me how to use it in context.

Sometimes it scares me to death to think that my kids are

shaped by watching my behavior. I'd much rather they do as I say, not do as I do. But there's no doubt my actions will always win out over my words.

> Do you like the person you're becoming? If not, might I suggest that you take a look at what's on the throne of your heart? Because one of the fundamental truths of human nature—and the greatest dangers of idolatry—is that what we worship shapes who we are.

It's not just children who learn through imitation though. The Bible teaches that all of us imitate something or somebody (1 Corin.). We reflect what we experience. We've been created to do that.

The only real question is this: *What—or who—will we imitate and reflect?*

Up to this point, this book has served as something of a diagnostic, a tool to help you see what may be serving as idols in your life. We all need to be prompted to tear down those "high places" and begin again. My prayer is that these last few chapters will serve as a sort of blueprint for what I believe God wants to erect in your life in place of those idols you've been carrying.

BECOMING WHAT YOU WORSHIP

Take a moment to evaluate your life. Do you like the person you're becoming? If not, might I suggest that you take a look at what's on the throne of your heart? Because one of the fundamental truths of human nature—and the greatest dangers of idolatry—is that what we worship shapes who we are.

Psalm 115 vividly warns of this danger in describing idolatrous nations:

> *But their idols are silver and gold,*
> *made by human hands.*
> *They have mouths, but cannot speak,*
> *eyes, but cannot see.*
> *They have ears, but cannot hear,*
> *noses, but cannot smell.*
> *They have hands, but cannot feel,*
> *feet, but cannot walk,*
> *nor can they utter a sound with their throats.*
> *Those who make them will be like them,*
> *and so will all who trust in them. (vv. 4–8)*

The psalmist is trying to paint a stark contrast by comparing the living God with the lifeless idols fashioned from wood and stone. Those who followed those idols, he says, had become spiritually lifeless, just like the blind, deaf, and mute pieces of metal they had crafted with their own hands.

The prophet Jeremiah made a similar statement regarding his faithless ancestors:

> *They followed worthless idols*
> *and became worthless themselves. (Jer. 2:5).*

His point applies to any of us today: *what we worship determines what we become.*

If we set our desires on anything other than the true God, we will become like that thing. Desire that is focused on the right object—the one true God—enables and grows a human being. Desire set on the wrong thing corrupts and debases us.

If we worship money, in other words, we'll become a greedy person.

If we worship sex, we'll become a lustful person.

If we worship power, we'll become a corrupt person.

If we worship accomplishment, we'll become a restless, frantic person.

If we worship love and acceptance, we'll become a slave to others.

If we worship external beauty, we'll become shallow.

And worshipping anything other than the true God will make us something other than what he created us to be.

LESS THAN HUMAN

I believe one of the reasons God so adamantly speaks out against idolatry throughout the Bible is that we simply can't worship something other than God and still live out our God-given purpose. What is that purpose? It's revealed in the very first chapter of the Bible:

> Then God said, "Let us make human beings in our image, to be like us. . . ."

> *So God created human beings in his own image,*
> *In the image of God he created them;*
> *male and female he created them. (Gen. 1:26–27 NLT)*

Our purpose, in other words, is to reflect the God who made us.

Not long ago I read an article by John Ortberg that brought a great deal of clarity to my mind concerning these verses. He wrote about an ancient belief that only kings were made in the image of a powerful God. Peasants or common folks were generally thought to be made in the image of inferior gods.[1]

But that's not what Genesis 1:26–27 tells us. In fact, it directly contradicts that ancient belief by claiming that *every* human being is made in the image of a powerful God.

This is a world-changing truth about human dignity and human value. Just imagine the liberation that it brought to the people who first heard it—and that it can bring to us. As Carolyn Custis James put it,

> We walk away yawning as though nothing all that important is happening here—unimpressed with the glorious identity God has just dropped in our laps. Given the fact that we've just heard one of the most startling announcements in all of history, it is remarkable that we do so little with this and must be somewhat disappointing to God that he doesn't get more of a reaction out of us. By naming us his image bearers, God has made a relationship with himself the strategic center of his purpose for humanity and for the world.[2]

But there is more to these two verses. The fact that we were made in the image of God tells us not just about our worth but also about our destiny. The main point of the "image of God" language in Scripture is not some ability or character trait we share with God. It's our mission in this world he has given us.

Ortberg's article points out that an ancient king who wanted people to know whose kingdom they were in would set up images of himself throughout the land. When you saw a particular king's image, you knew for a fact that you were in that king's territory. "Genesis is saying that just as a king would place images of himself around so people would know who was ruling, 'So God has placed his own image, human beings, into his world so that the world can see who its ruler is.'"[3]

> The fact that we were made in the image of God tells us not just about our worth but also about our destiny.

N. T. Wright created a beautiful picture of how this works:

Imagine God up above, the earth below. In between them, human
beings are set at a 45 degree angle with a mirror.

Your job, your destiny, is to reflect the holy reign of God
down on to the earth—to care for all of creation and particularly human beings the way God would want you to;

And then to gather up all the goodness and delight of the
earth and put it into words and offer it to God in worship.

Your destiny is to contribute more creative God-given goodness to the earth than you can currently imagine; And to offer
more earthy joy and gratitude to God than you can currently
contain.[4]

The bottom line is that ultimately God made humans to reflect
him. But if we don't seek him above all things, we'll end up reflecting something else in creation—something lesser. In the process,
we'll lose our true humanity.

Isn't this the story told in Romans 1?

The wrath of God is being revealed from heaven against all the
godlessness and wickedness of people, who suppress the truth by
their wickedness . . .

For although they knew God, they neither glorified him as
God nor gave thanks to him, but their thinking became futile
and their foolish hearts were darkened. Although they claimed
to be wise, they became fools and exchanged the glory of the
immortal God for images made to look like a mortal human
being and birds and animals and reptiles.

Therefore God gave them over in the sinful desires of their
hearts to sexual impurity for the degrading of their bodies with
one another. They exchanged the truth about God for a lie, and
worshiped and served created things rather than the Creator. (vv.
18, 21–25)

Instead of worshipping the Creator, the people Paul was describing worshipped his creatures. And what happened as a result? Did they become nobler? No. They became degraded and animalistic—as well as deluded. Their misdirected worship didn't enable these people or elevate them. It simply made them less human.

Our ability to fulfill our purpose on this earth is dramatically diminished when we worship idols of any kind instead of our God and Father. But we *find* our purpose when we worship the one true God. When we declare our allegiance to him with all that we are and all that we have, we begin to reflect in our lives the character qualities of the One we worship and admire. In the process we find ourselves becoming more truly human.

But for this to happen, we may need to make sure the God we're worshipping really is the one true God.

PERCEPTION AND REFLECTION

I grew up on Central Avenue here in Nashville, Tennessee. To this day it's one of my favorite streets in the city. Now zoned as historic, it's full of bungalow homes with big front porches shaded by lots of beautiful, mature trees scattered throughout. I've got some great memories of that neighborhood—including a time when I learned an indelible lesson about my perceptions.

Do you remember a time when almost every neighborhood used to have at least one home that had been determined by the kids to be haunted? We had one of those. It was occupied by a family I'll call the Porters. That wasn't their real name, but I think it's best to use a pseudonym, because we kids were completely convinced that the Porters were all ax murderers. And we had proof!

There was the time we saw a man standing in the Porters' window holding a knife, with what looked like blood all over his hands and arms. Another time we saw the family unloading what we were sure was a dead body out of their fifteen-passenger van and carrying it down the basement stairs into their home. And the final straw for us was the day we were playing in the back alley and saw guys dressed up in all black, with painted faces, practicing what seemed to be some sort of military drill.

My friends in the neighborhood were typical boys, which means we were always daring each other to do things: "I dare you to jump out of that tree." Or, "I dare you to eat that worm." Or even, "I dare you to ride your bike across the Porters' front yard."

One day I got the ultimate of all dares—to run up and touch the Porters' front door. I was terrified. But turning down a dare at that age could devastate a reputation. So with all of the courage I could muster, I took off running. I raced across their yard, up the daunting front steps, and onto their large, shaded porch. But in my haste I tripped over the top step and went crashing right into their front door.

Before I could gather myself back up and get the heck out of there, Mrs. Porter opened the front door. At this point she was about seventy years old and all of about four-foot-eight. And she was laughing—so hard that her entire body was shaking. Apparently she had been standing there for some time, watching us put our elaborate plan together.

That day was a breakthrough. The Porters would actually become good friends with my family, and we would eventually discover that they were not ax murderers at all. They owned a film company and often used their house as a movie set. That explained most if not all of the suspicious activity we had carefully observed.

What I learned that day is something that I've noticed many times since then: our relationships are formed by our perceptions of each other. And this applies not only to our relationships with one another, but also to our relationship with God.

A. W. Tozer once wrote, "What comes into our minds when we think about God is the most important thing about us."[5]

It doesn't get any more essential than this. You see, it's not enough just to worship God so you can reflect God. You've got to worship an accurate picture of God so you reflect an accurate image of God.

Have you ever known Christians to do outlandish things in the "name of God"?

Several months ago I learned via a phone call that a famous—or infamous—religious group was going to be picketing at our Cross Point Nashville campus. This Kansas-based group was well-known for showing up at churches, public gatherings, and even funerals with what I consider to be vulgar signs condemning anyone who doesn't share their *very* narrow view of God. Some of the signs I've seen on the news have proclaimed:

- "Thank God for 9/11."
- "God hates fags."
- "God hates Jews."
- "You're going to hell."

As it turned out, they never showed up at our church, so I don't know what they would have said about us. But I think about this particular group often. You see, I think they really believe that what they're doing is noble. In their minds they're representing God and doing this world a favor by communicating his message. The problem, in my opinion, is that it's absolutely the wrong message—based on a completely misguided picture of God.

> It's not enough just to worship God so you can reflect God. You've got to worship an accurate picture of God so you reflect an accurate image of God.

Unfortunately, they're not the only ones to do such a thing. Many of us harbor an inaccurate and damaging picture of God—in effect, a false god.

If we imagine a God who wants to meet all the desires of our ego-driven, self-centered, materialistic lives, we're worshipping a false god.

If we imagine a God who is nothing but an overindulgent parent who will give us anything we want if we ask nicely, we're worshipping a false god.

If we imagine a God who withholds his love and waits for us to submit to a system of rules to earn that love, we're worshipping a false god.

And what happens when we do that? Every misconception about God carries a corresponding consequence in terms of our relationship with him and others.

Do you see God as a cosmic cop waiting for you and others to screw up? If so, you may spend your life walking on eggshells.

Do you see him as an impatient father withholding his love from you until you finally become "good enough"? You may never stop jumping through hoops, trying to make him happy.

Do you see him as a heavenly concierge whose main concern is your comfort? You may resent him for not doing his job.

Do you believe he thinks and acts like you? Chances are, you'll be confused most of the time, trying to figure out his next move.

Having an accurate and biblical view of God is important because idolatry is a sin that has its beginning in the mind—in thoughts, beliefs, judgments, and imagination.

Incorrect thinking about God's character is always a catalyst to idolatry.

THE ROAD OUT OF IDOLATRY

I once heard someone say that you can't just relinquish an idol. You have to replace it.

In other words, we can't just say, "I want to stop caring so much about accomplishment in my life" or, "I'm going to stop being a control freak."

Well, we can *say* those things, but saying them probably won't stop our idolatrous behavior—because as soon as we abandon one empty promise, our hearts will gravitate toward another one. And another.

That is, unless we make the conscious choice to shift the focus of our worship—to replace a false god with the real One.

If I want to remove the idol of approval, for instance, I have to focus on God's love as well as the worth and value that he gave me through the simple act of creation.

If I want to remove the idol of money, I have to start focusing on God's generosity and his compelling commands to give instead of receive, which break the pattern of get, get, get, in my life.

In other words, breaking the pattern of idolatry in our lives requires not only a "turn from" but a "turn to."

We can't just *stop* worshipping a certain idol.

We have to *start* actively worshipping God.

Worshipping him continually reminds us it's about *his* power, not ours. It's about *his* purposes, not ours. It's about *his* glory, not ours.

If it's true that we become like what we worship, the road out of idolatry is to give up on all those empty promises and start trusting the living God. In psychological language, we must "detach" and then "reattach."

But this can come only by God's gracious intervention. Willpower will not do it. Moral conviction will not do it. Only brokenness at the center of our beings will do it. Only surrender will do it. Only letting the love of Jesus cut through our shame and guilt will do it.

The ability to renounce idolatry is God's gift. It's what enables us to begin our true worship of the true God. Paul makes this point in Romans 12:1: "Therefore, I urge you, brothers and sisters, *in view of God's mercy*, to offer your bodies as a living sacrifice, holy and pleasing to God—this is your true and proper worship" (italics mine).

God's mercy comes first. According to the previous eleven chapters of Romans, mercy means his free grace and justification, given to us in the death of his Son and sealed in our hearts by his Spirit. It is only by this mercy that we can come to worship.

What do we do in response? We worship. That is, we bring the sacrifice of ourselves—made acceptable by the sacrifice of Christ—and ask God to fill the "hole in our souls" with himself. We make the choice to turn to him, to love him with all our hearts, minds, souls, and strengths. We fall down before him as King. We offer him our gifts: our shouts of joy, our songs of praise, our tithes and offerings. Worship becomes witness as we confess all that Jesus has done for us. We bring our petitions, listen for his voice, and trust him to answer our prayers. Then we move forward into obedience, which is the joyful living out of his will for us.

The whole purpose of worship is to change us into Christlikeness. Rather than being conformed to this world, we reject the empty promises and our idolatrous addictions. Then Christ in turn conforms us to himself (Rom. 12:2). He begins to birth in us the character we've been missing.

Do you see how it all works? We leave our idols. We come to Jesus. We surrender to him. And he changes us, more and more. He re-creates us in his image and creates in us what Richard Foster has termed a "holy dependency."[6] We become utterly and completely dependent upon God for anything significant to happen in our lives.

It was a holy dependency that led Isaiah to see God for who he truly was and cry out, "Woe to me! . . . I am ruined! For I am a man of unclean lips, and I live among a people of unclean lips, and my eyes have seen the King, the LORD Almighty" (Isa. 6:5).

Putting God in his proper place in our minds and hearts allows us to put everything else into perspective, including the things we're often tempted to look to for what only God can give us. That's why worship is one of our most powerful defenses against the empty promises of idolatry.

WORSHIP IS A WAY OF LIFE

I think for years I defined worship as something that happened during a set of four songs on a Sunday morning. I limited worship to something that required someone on stage with a guitar to lead me into. People from a different tradition or time might similarly limit worship to singing from hymnals while an organ plays or sitting quietly on pews and waiting for the Spirit to move. But I've come to believe that all of these "churchy" definitions of worship are far too limiting.

Worship can be practiced with each and every breath we take. Don't make the mistake of worshipping God one day a week and totally

> Without worship, my life quickly shrivels into insignificant moments, purposeless living, and meaningless idol worship that leave me longing and lost.

missing him the other six days. Don't make the mistake of acknowledging his presence for thirty minutes during your morning quiet time and than ignoring him the other twenty-three hours and thirty minutes left in your day.

Hebrews 13:15 tells us, "Through Jesus, therefore, let us *continually* offer to God a sacrifice of praise" (italics mine).

Worship can happen while I'm driving down the road.

Worship can happen when I stop and stare at the stars in the sky.

Worship can happen as I raise my voice to him alongside others.

Worship can happen while I'm watching my kids play.

Worship can happen any moment of any day because it's simply my response to who God is and what he has done. It's my acknowledgment that what I'm searching for comes from him and him alone.

I'm learning that I can't limit my worship to music or buildings, to contemporary or traditional, or to just Sunday. If I want to get serious about transformation, I have to get serious about worship—and understand that it's a way of life. Without worship, my life quickly shrivels into insignificant moments, purposeless living, and meaningless idol worship that leave me longing and lost.

When I'm regularly engaging in worship, I'm constantly reminded that there is an infinite, all-powerful, limitless God who is drawing me into his presence, where I'm constantly being shaped by his ever-present grace into something that resembles him more and more.

This worship gives me power when I'm weak, patience when I hurry, love when I'm angry, peace when I fret, and hope when I want to give up.

While he holds entire galaxies in the very palm of his hand and has simply thought us humans into existence, giving us life and breath and all things, he also invites you and me to enter into relationship with him, beholding him as he is so that we may become the men and women we so desire to be.

He invites us with each and every breath to remember that there is no other God. That there is a connection between his infinite worth, discovered in the practice and discipline of worship, and our own inner longing to love something supremely.

It's only when we open our hearts to truly worship our Creator that we are set free to release the small gods who pretend to wield such power.

Empty promises are just that. Empty.

No other God can compare.

CHAPTER ELEVEN
LIVING CLOSE TO TRUTH

I've spent most of my afternoon today in one counseling meeting after another.

There was the guy whose wife has left him because he's devoted his entire life to climbing the ladder. She was finally fed up with taking care of the kids and all the family needs while he continued to cheat his family for the corporate dream. He told me there were plenty of signs along the way that he was doing immense damage at home, but he ignored them to pursue what he thought he wanted more than anything. Now that his family is gone, he realizes he has lost what matters to him most.

There was the couple who are hitting rock bottom right now because they're going to lose their house, give up their cars, and file bankruptcy. In their desire to keep up with their friends, they maxed out their credit, buying stuff they didn't need with money they didn't have in order to impress people they didn't even like. When the husband lost his job a couple of months ago, it all came caving in.

I could go on and on and tell you the three or four other scenarios I faced this afternoon, but they're all tied together by a common thread: self-deception.

We've touched on the idea that human beings have an uncanny propensity for fooling ourselves. And if you think this isn't a problem for you, then chances are you are my number one example. Because the truth is, we're all deceived by something.

Of course, the very nature of self-deception makes it easier to see it in the lives of other people than in ourselves.

You know what I mean. You've probably had friends whose lives spiraled out of control before your eyes. You wanted to pull your hair out as they made the same mistakes over and over.

You knew that guy was bad news for her.

You knew that job was controlling him.

You knew that their "enough is never enough" mentality was going to wreck them.

It was all so obvious to you, but they couldn't see it. And if it happens to your friends from time to time, I'm sure it's happening to you as well.

The Bible warns us of such deception in Galatians 6:7–8: "Do not be deceived: God cannot be mocked. A man reaps what he sows. Whoever sows to please their flesh, from the flesh will reap destruction; whoever sows to please the Spirit, from the Spirit will reap eternal life."

Proverbs 14:12 suggests the same thing:

> *There is a way that appears to be right,*
> *but in the end it leads to death.*

Can there be any clearer example of "a way that . . . leads to death" than depending on the deception—and self-deception—of an empty promise?

The question throughout this book has not been, "Do you struggle with idolatry?" We established early on that we all do. And we've spent a great deal of time trying to identify some of the common empty promises people in our culture struggle with. My guess is that one or more of them sound familiar to you. They certainly do to me.

The million-dollar question now becomes, "What do we do about our idols?" How can we become increasingly aware of the things that lure our hearts away from Jesus and delude us into thinking they can provide our lives with meaning and significance and success?

We've already looked at some answers:

> Simply identifying our idols and wanting to replace them probably won't lead to any kind of personal transformation. What we really need is a way to experience God daily so we can continually break through the self-deception and realize just how lifeless and empty our idols are.

- realizing we have idolatrous hearts
- identifying what people or things we tend to look to give us what only God can give us
- understanding these idols cannot just simply be removed but must be replaced
- replacing our idols with God himself
- finding ourselves in worship

In all of this, it's important to recognize that simply identifying our idols and wanting to replace them probably won't lead to any kind of personal transformation. What we really need is a way to experience God daily so we can continually break through the self-deception and realize just how lifeless and empty our idols are.

It takes a living encounter with the living God to keep us living close to the truth.

There are certain spiritual practices that allow me to see more clearly the truth about myself, my desires, and the lies I've believed. They help me have that living encounter with a holy God that I need so desperately. I've learned that apart from these habits, or disciplines, I succumb more easily to a state of deception that leads to idolatry. I pray these brief discussions will serve as an invitation for you to discover—or rediscover—the abundant life that comes with putting Jesus in the center of your life.

SOLITUDE

In June 2000 I was going through some difficult times in ministry. I wasn't really depressed or angry or burned out. I just felt uninspired, mediocre, and stuck. I didn't have a real vision for what God wanted me to do next, and I felt that my spiritual growth had stalled.

I had heard of other pastors who would go away for "silence and solitude" retreats. At the end of my rope, I decided that this sounded like a good idea. Nothing else seemed to be working, so why not?

A family in the church had a small cabin in a place called Leonard Oak, Kentucky. I think there are fewer than a dozen people who actually know where Leonard Oak is. I think fewer than a dozen people live there too. I decided it might be a good place for my solitary retreat.

I pulled up to the little cabin, all excited about what God might do in my life over the next twenty-four hours. I had a portable CD player with me with a dozen or so messages I wanted to listen to. I had my computer, several books, some music, and a variety of other things to keep me entertained.

And yes, I can see the flaw in my reasoning . . . now.

While I was technically alone for those twenty-four hours, there was very little silence or any real solitude, for that matter. I had brought plenty of things to keep my mind distracted. But still, I was miserable for most of the time. I had this gnawing urge to return as quickly as possible to "productivity." The idea of sitting and being silent before God felt pointless, even impossible. I had to keep fighting the urge to get on the phone and get something done.

Now why would a simple solitary weekend be so difficult for me? For the same reason you probably organize your life, consciously or unconsciously, to avoid being quiet or alone for very long. Quite simply, I was scared.

I don't think there's any question that many of us are addicted to noise, driven to eradicate all silence. As Dallas Willard put it,

> Silence is frightening because it strips us as nothing else does, throwing us upon the stark realities of our life. It reminds us of death, which will cut us off from this world and leave only us and God. And in that quiet, what if there turns out to be very little to "us and God"?[1]

That's it exactly! That's what I feared—being stripped, being exposed. I also didn't want to face the fact that I had allowed myself to be shaped more by what I do or what others think of me than by my Creator.

Henri Nouwen, writing of his own experience with solitude, beautifully summarized both the challenges and the benefits of solitude and silence:

> In solitude I get rid of my scaffolding; no friends to talk with, no telephone calls to make, no meetings to attend, no music to entertain, no books to distract, just me—naked, vulnerable, weak, sinful, deprived, broken—nothing. It is this nothingness that I have to face in my solitude, a nothingness so dreadful that

everything in me wants to run to my friends, my work, and my distractions so that I can forget my nothingness and make myself believe that I am worth something. But that is not all. As soon as I decide to stay in my solitude, confusing ideas, disturbing images, wild fantasies, and weird associations jump about in my mind like monkeys in a banana tree. Anger and greed begin to show their ugly faces. I give long, hostile speeches to my enemies and dream lustful dreams in which I am wealthy, influential, and very attractive—or poor, ugly, and in need of immediate consolation. Thus I try again to run from the dark abyss of my nothingness and restore my false self in all its vainglory.

The task is to persevere in my solitude, to stay in my cell until all my seductive visitors get tired of pounding on my door and leave me alone.[2]

Despite the fear and the challenges, I believe that solitude is something we all need. It was certainly important for Jesus. According to Luke 5:16, "Jesus often withdrew to lonely places and prayed." Luke does not quantify the word *often*, but his words indicate that Jesus withdrew into solitude to be with God at regular intervals.

Now, if Jesus Christ, the Son of God, thought it was important and necessary to withdraw to be with the Father, how much more important is it for you and me?

We long for a place where our deep yearning to be loved unconditionally can be met. We long for a place where we can rest from our out-of-control, hectic, day-to-day world. We long for a place where we can be reminded that our lives really do matter and can count for something disproportionate to who we are.

Solitude is that place. It is where we finally have a chance to let down our guards and encounter our Lord without distraction. Just you or me—alone with the One who offers us real love and satisfaction.

FASTING

I have to be honest here. I haven't always been a happy faster. In fact, I hated fasting when I first started this practice. I didn't understand it, and I totally dreaded the fasts I undertook. And yet I can also say with honesty that fasting has become an extremely important discipline to me, something that helps me uncover my empty promises and identify the roots of idolatry in my life.

Fasting reminds me of my humanness. It shows me what I really need and what I really desire. It nudges me to remember just how much I need to remain connected to the life-giving source that is Jesus Christ. With each hunger pain, with each desire I have to run back to something I have depended on, I'm prompted to seek out intimacy with the One who truly sustains me.

I remember asking a friend if he had ever fasted. He said, "Heck no. Why would I do that? I love food, and there is absolutely nothing wrong with food. Why would I abstain from it as if there were something inherently evil in it?"

But he was missing the whole point—just as I once did.

Fasting isn't just going without food—though fasting from food can be a useful practice. Fasting is a voluntary abstinence from *anything* that could possibly stand in the way of connecting to Christ from moment to moment—whatever that may be. You can fast from anything, from sodas to cell phones.

The focus of a fast is not what is ridiculously evil, but what is deceptively good.

And fasting isn't about ridding your life of evil. In fact, many of the things we fast from are good things, even gifts from God, though they may have progressively become too important to us. It seems to me that we have an undeniable propensity toward becoming obsessed and maybe even addicted to activities and objects that ultimately have little meaning—shopping, novels, TV and video games, e-mail, Facebook, Twitter, the Internet in general.

At any rate, it's important to recognize that the focus of a fast is not what is ridiculously evil, but what is deceptively good. John Piper wrote,

> The greatest enemy of hunger for God is not poison but apple pie. It is not the banquet of the wicked that dulls our appetite for heaven, but endless nibbling at the table of the world. It is not the X-rated video, but the prime-time dribble of triviality we drink in every night. For all the ill that Satan can do, when God describes what keeps us from the banquet table of his love, it is a piece of land, a yoke of oxen, and a wife (Luke 14:18–20). The greatest adversary of love to God is not his enemies but his gifts. And the most deadly appetites are not for the poison of evil, but for the simple pleasures of earth. For when these replace an appetite for God himself, the idolatry is scarcely recognizable, and almost incurable.[3]

One of the most rewarding and yet difficult fasts in my life these days is my weekly technology fast. For twenty-four hours I do my best to abstain from television, phones, Internet, Facebook, Twitter, and the like. Instead I spent my time reading, praying, playing with my family, and generally slowing down long enough to notice the amazing gifts God has blessed me with.

Don't get me wrong. I love technology. I love how it keeps me connected to people around the world. I love the many ways I can communicate and share and learn and be challenged through my cell phone, iPad, laptop, and more. But I'm slowly learning there is a difference between using technology and being used by technology or even making it an idol. My fast helps me remember that difference.

Fasting from technology has proved more difficult than I ever imagined. But every time I grab for the cell phone or run in to check Facebook, I'm prompted to pause and pray—which is the real point of fasting. This discipline had been an incredible catalyst for me to realize how quickly I fill my life with things other than the pursuit of God.

We all have this tendency to fill up the empty spaces in our lives with whatever is easily at hand, and this makes it difficult to know what we're really hungry for. We have this illusion of satisfaction that comes along with our relative affluence, our busy lives, and our often-fake spirituality.

I've been amazed over the course of my twenty-five years as a Christian just how often and easily I seem to deceive myself spiritually. I have a truly impressive ability to sound so much more spiritual than I actually am. I'm quick to praise God with my lips, to announce that he's the most important thing in my life, to claim that everything in this world pales in comparison to him.

Fasting allows me to put those meaningless words to the test. It reveals just how easily I deceive myself into thinking that God is the most important thing in my life when in reality I am eyeball deep in idolatry.

Richard Foster made this point in *Celebration of Discipline*:

> More than any other Discipline, fasting reveals the things that control us. This is a wonderful benefit to the true disciple who longs to be transformed into the image of Jesus Christ. We cover up what is inside of us with food and other good things.[4]

In Psalm 35:13, David said, "I . . . humbled myself with fasting." But what does humbling our souls have to do with fasting? I've found that in fasting I quickly become aware of what is within us—the sexual temptations, the bitterness in certain relationships, the fears of failure, the unresolved anger, the jealousy that bubbles just beneath the surface, the unsatisfied yearnings—and I realize just how much I desperately need God's healing power in my life. I realize how I desperately need to live from one moment to the next in his presence, which fulfills my soul hunger in a way none of these empty promises ever will.

Few spiritual disciplines are as countercultural as fasting. I think few would argue with me that our culture's voice continually screams, "More is better." Marketing seems to dominate us 24/7, encouraging us to focus on what we *don't* have (or think we don't have)—money, power, sex, beauty, whatever.

Fasting helps turn our minds and hearts back to what we do have—and what we really need. It's based on the idea that we need less of something in order to have more of the most important thing. It's a way to pause from the endless and mindless consumption that engulfs us almost before we're aware of it and to relearn what Jesus himself taught us: "Is not life more than food, and the body more than clothes?" (Matt. 6:25).

Fasting is paradoxical. I embrace emptiness in order to experience fullness. When I fast, I'm hoping that in my emptiness I will more readily recognize God as the source of all human life and activity. In my emptiness I have a heightened awareness of my dependence on God.

In so many ways I can't explain, fasting puts me in a position to not only hear from God but to be formed by God. It takes me to a place where I feel a heightened sense of vulnerability and a diminished sense of power. I've come to believe that equates to a certain availability to hear and obey God.

My experience is that when I surround myself with all of the things that make me comfortable, I require little if any power from God. Surrounded with everything I think I need, involved with my own means, methods, strategies, and plans, I become a product of my own will and wisdom.

But fasting from any or all of these things helps shatter my soul's arrogance. It leaves my body and soul crying out in hunger for God. And that's a hunger that really can be filled.

GOD'S WORD

Who would have ever imagined twenty years ago that the storage-unit business would end up being a billion-dollar industry? The typical American has accumulated so much stuff, we have to pay to store the overflow.

What's interesting is that we've each been created with a mental storage unit as well—our brains. But while the storage capacity of the human brain is quite large, it's not infinite. And most of us find our mental storerooms cluttered from the constant barrage of "content" we are bombarded with.

It's widely reported that the average person is bombarded with some three thousand marketing messages a day. While there is some debate on the number,[5] no one disputes that normal life for most Americans includes a constant barrage of messages that are strategically designed to create a vision of the good life:

- "Eat this."
- "Drive this."
- "Say this."
- "Wear this."
- "Think this."
- "Spend this."
- "Buy this."

In each and every case, the good life supposedly requires whatever product or service the marketing masters happen to be offering. Whether we're aware of it or not, these messages and images are

piling up in our mental storage units. And—this is the really important point—all of that stuff we store in our brains affects the way we
think and act.

Jesus had a few things to say about how this works.

> Make a tree good and its fruit will be good, or make a tree bad and
> its fruit will be bad, for a tree is recognized by its fruit. You brood
> of vipers, how can you who are evil say anything good? For the
> mouth speaks what the heart is full of. A good man brings good
> things out of the good stored up in him, and an evil man brings
> evil things out of the evil stored up in him. (Matt. 12:33–35)

The principle here is pretty obvious. If what you can't see, the
inside of the tree, is healthy, then the fruit, the stuff you can see,
will be healthy also. If the inside is bad, then the fruit is going to
be bad.

You see, Jesus' ultimate goal was not to create a list of rules that
would help us live a better life. He understood that spiritual transformation is all about internal changes that will eventually affect the
way you live. It's about choosing what we accumulate in our mental
storage units.

This principle is why I believe it's so essential for me to immerse
myself in Scripture. It's my way of storing up "good things" in my
mind and heart. I'm aware of a profound need to have the words of
God feed my soul and teach me all the things that I should know.

Paul encourages us all to do just this. He wrote, "Be transformed
by the renewing of your mind" (Rom. 12:2).

These days I like to view God's Word and my practice of reading
it daily as a time where I open up my hands and receive the gifts that
God desires to give me. It's an opportunity for his grace and love to
surprise me. It's an opportunity to allow my mind to be renewed and
transformed, filled to the brim with good things that can't help but

come out and influence my life. As I dwell on its beauty, ponder its meaning, and explore its implications, I'm reminded of how God and only God can meet the desires I long for.

PRAYER

An effective prayer life is an essential part of fighting back against idolatry. It's something we all desperately need yet often neglect. In fact, Christians often feel guiltier about their prayer lives—or lack of prayer lives—than almost any other aspect of their spiritual lives.

How about you? Ever feel guilty about how little time you spend in prayer or about not being able to stay focused during prayer time? Ever wonder if you're praying the right way or worry that you should be doing something different?

John Ortberg wrote about this in his book *The Me I Want to Be*:

> When I pray, I end up praying about things I think I *should* be concerned about: missionaries, world peace, and global warming. But my mind keeps wandering toward stuff I am genuinely concerned about. The way to let my talking flow into praying is this: *I must pray what is in me, not what I wish were in me.*[6]

I love that. What an incredible breakthrough. The more I've started to pray what's in me instead of what I wish were in me, the more I've been able to truly enjoy my time with God.

This really gets into a deeper issue of prayer. I think many of us live with this idea that somehow God doesn't hear or see certain things in our lives. We actually think we can fool God by praying about one thing even though we're thinking and focused on another. (Here comes that self-deception again.)

Sometimes I have to laugh as I watch my three boys fight at dinner over who's going to ask the blessing.

It usually starts with my oldest, Jett, saying something like, "I think Gage should pray tonight." Gage will say, "No, I think Brewer should pray." And Brewer will say, "No, I prayed last night. It's Jett's turn."

Just a few nights ago I asked my son Gage if he would bless the food. He looked at me with these big puppy-dog eyes and said, "Dad, I want to. I really do. But I'm just way too hungry to pray tonight. Someone else is going to have to do it."

The excuses will typically go on and on until I finally step in and assign someone this most difficult task of thanking God for the food he has provided for us. Then one of the boys will actually launch into a prayer that will make you think he's wanted to do that all day.

The whole routine is not only funny, but quite ironic, because apparently it never crosses those boys' minds that maybe God can actually hear them arguing about not wanting to pray. But no adult would ever think that way. Right?

Sure we would. We do it all the time.

This is exactly why people use a different voice when they pray! It's why we think we have to close our eyes or be in a certain position with our hands held just right. It's why we pray about stuff we think sounds spiritual instead of just saying what's truly on our hearts and minds.

You will experience a breakthrough in your prayer life when you discover you don't have to pray anything other than what's on your mind and in your heart. This is when you begin to discover that every moment, every thought, every second is another opportunity to connect with your Father in heaven.

My fear is that this issue with prayer is just an indicator of a much larger concern—our tendency to separate our spiritual lives from our everyday lives. It's why you talk one way when you're at church and another way when you're at work. It's why you act one way when you're with your friends at Bible study and another when you're with your friends at the mall or on the golf course.

To rid ourselves of idolatry, we have to move beyond compartmentalizing God into one particular section of our lives. And that is especially true when it comes to prayer.

Prayer was never intended to be an activity. It's more of an ongoing conversation, a way of being in relationship.

Do you remember learning to drive? I still remember it as though it was yesterday. My father, like so many dads, made me learn on a stick shift. I remember sitting down in the driver's seat and being overwhelmed by the list of things I had to do:

- Turn the key.
- Check the mirrors.
- Adjust the seat just right.
- Place both hands on the wheel and take a deep breath.
- Press down as hard as I can on the brake pedal.
- Slowly press the clutch all the way in.
- Reach down and put the car in first gear.
- Immediately place my right hand back on the wheel.
- Slowly take my foot off the brake and at the same time start to let the clutch out.
- Apply the gas as I start to feel the car shake violently.
- Jerk forward and hope the car doesn't die.

For weeks, maybe even months, this was the mental checklist I would run through every time I got in the car. I don't remember at what point I stopped thinking through these steps and just started to drive. But these days I can jump in my car and accomplish the whole thing while carrying on a conversation. I don't even have to think about it.

I think this is how prayer should be. Not that it becomes a meaningless routine, but that somehow we shift from compartmentalized prayers to making prayer a natural and habitual part of our lives. Somehow we move away from *I'm sitting here with my eyes closed praying, and now I'm typing at work, and now I'm praying again, and now I'm hanging out with friends, and now I'm praying.* Instead, prayer becomes an integral part of the way we live.

Just think about this handful of places in Scripture that describe prayer as something almost as natural as breathing:

- "Jesus told his disciples a parable to show them that they should *always* pray and not give up" (Luke 18:1, italics mine).
- "Pray in the Spirit *on all occasions* . . . *always* keep on praying" (Eph. 6:18, italics mine).
- "Pray *continually*" (1 Thess. 5:17, italics mine).

Again, these verses point to prayer as being something so much more than sitting down and closing our eyes and praying through some list of things we want God to change. It becomes a way for us to continually be aware of the presence of God. As Ortberg put it,

> The goal of prayer is not to get good at praying, as many people think. The goal of prayer is not to try to set new records for how much time we spend praying. *The goal of prayer is to live all my life and speak all of my words in the joyful awareness of the presence of God.*[7]

Do you understand what this means?

Prayer is not thinking about God in contrast to thinking about other things like sports. Prayer isn't even spending time with God in contrast to spending time with other people. When you separate God from such things, you begin to separate God from your daily life and cut off the necessary connection of you from Jesus. In the language of John 15:1–17, you're cutting off the branch (you) from the Vine (Jesus).

I'm learning that every moment is a moment for prayer because every moment is a moment to be aware of God's presence. And this discipline of constant prayer is an opportunity to be awakened to God with us.

Does all this mean I should never set aside a specific time to pray? Not at all. After all, I had to practice driving a lot before it became natural to me, and I still have to pay attention to what I'm doing when I drive. Regular prayer times, alone or in community, help us focus on God's presence without distraction and deepen our relationship with him, just as set-aside times of togetherness can deepen a marriage. Setting aside dedicated time for prayer also helps us guard against the self-deception of claiming we're "praying on the fly" when we're really just going about our business with only passing thoughts about God.

I would never counsel you *not* to have a regular dedicated prayer time. But I've come to believe that the habit formed by the deliberate practice of prayer is more a means to an end than an end in itself. We practice praying to help us make prayer an integral part of our lives.

I had the opportunity a few weeks ago to play golf with Max Lucado. Max has been a hero of mine since I was in college, and I jumped at the opportunity to hang out with him for the day. As we stepped on the first tee box, I heard him say something that was so simple and yet so profound. As he stood there practicing his warm-up swing, he just looked toward heaven and said, "God, thank you for this beautiful day to play golf."

This simple act was profound to me because I realized Max was taking the opportunity to reconnect with the presence of God and usher himself into an awareness that *God is present in this very moment.* Even standing on a tee box he is present and responsible for this amazing day we've been given.

I believe that is the ultimate goal of prayer—from moment to moment, to be connected to an awareness of the presence of God. To stay grafted onto the Vine, because without that life supply we lose the power we so desperately need to avoid the empty promises of this world. To acknowledge God's presence as my source of life and power by presenting my thoughts, whatever they may be, to him. Or, as Henri Nouwen memorably put it, to "turn our perpetual mental activities into perpetual prayer" and get to the point where "thinking become[s] praying."[8]

> It is our time with him—not the spiritual practices that bring us to him—that shapes us more and more into the image of God originally planted within us even before our very existences.

Prayer is my opportunity to remember and reflect and, most importantly, just be conscious of Emmanuel—*God with us.* A God who is able and willing to help me live the life he's designed for me to live.

A WORD OF WARNING

Let me share with you my biggest fear with this chapter. I'm afraid that instead of allowing God to use the spiritual disciplines of solitude, Scripture, prayer, and fasting to counter our self-deceptions and transform us into people who love God and neighbor, we'll begin to polish and perfect these practices until they resemble bright, shiny, golden calves. When we do that, we block their power to transform us into the image of Christ. We may even begin to see the practices themselves as the mode of transformation, thus looking to them to give us what only God can give us.

It's quite possible to incorporate all the practices we've discussed and many others and have them do nothing to change your heart and mind. Not only is it possible; it's a reality for thousands of Christians every day.

So even as I encourage you to explore these disciplines, let me remind you that in and of themselves, these disciplines have no value! And if you're not careful, they could easily become idols.

Be careful not to allow the practice of spiritual disciplines to turn into, "See what I'm doing for you, God?" This is a subtle temptation that can wreck the work God wants to do in your life. It's easy to fall for the deception that if we do all the right things—that is, praying, fasting, reading the Word, seeking out solitude—God should bless us, take care of us, and meet all our ego-driven, self-centered needs.

Be careful, too, not to allow these spiritual practices to become nothing more than duty-driven religious activities. Don't take this light yoke Jesus has given us and turn it into a heavy burden for yourself and others.

If you start feeling guilty because you've missed your prayer time or skipped reading the Bible one day or got hungry and broke your fast, you're totally missing the point. This is not about you failing God or his being unhappy with you for your lack of trying.

Spiritual disciplines don't earn you "brownie points" with God. You don't earn God's love or favor by praying or reading the Bible or fasting or seeking solitude. These practices are simply ways to help you draw closer to him, to be more aware of his presence—to be with him and become more like him.

While there is a certain aspect of "doing" in these spiritual disciplines—finding a place to be alone, picking up a Bible to read, arranging your life so that fasting is possible, turning your prayerful attention toward God—we don't do them just for doing's sake. We do in order to be, performing these actions and making these choices so that we can be more easily ushered into the presence of God.

It is our time with him—not the spiritual practices that bring us to him—that shapes us more and more into the image of God originally planted within us even before our very existences. Spiritual disciplines are only a means to transformation, not the transformation itself.

In fact, I would go as far as to say that the goal here is not to try harder but to realize how useless our striving is.

Maybe the goal is to find ways, within these disciplines, to open ourselves more fully to what only God can do: transform us by his grace and truth.

CHAPTER TWELVE
SOUL SATISFACTION

Superman has always been my favorite superhero.

He wasn't the only one I had to choose from. Thanks to cartoons and comic books, I had a myriad of mighty men to identify with. But Superman was my number one choice. When I was a kid, I'd take every chance I could get to sit in front of the TV and watch him come to the rescue. He was always just in time to save the day.

As I write this we're headed into another blockbuster summer with a whole list of superhero movies about to come out. My boys are already begging me to see every one of them. Every time one of the previews comes on TV, my kids start screaming, "Dad, come in here! You have to see this! Dad, get in here now!"

This past Friday night I took my oldest son, Jett, to see the newest superhero flick. It was fun to watch his eyes light up as the movie jumped from scene to scene. He walked out of the theater with a huge smile on his face. And when I asked him what he thought about the movie, he said, "I loved it, Dad. I want to do something cool like that with my life."

I think my ten-year-old nailed the exact reason these stories continue to carry over from generation to generation.

Just think about it. It's basically the same story told over and over again, but it always seems to work. Whether it's Superman, Spider-Man, Wonder Woman, or the Power Rangers (my five-year-old made me add that), they all fit a very specific pattern. Some ordinary person is living an ordinary and somewhat boring everyday life, when something happens that changes everything. All of a sudden that ordinary person is something special.

Why? Well, typically there's some kind of gift or power involved. But it's more than that, isn't it? What's really different is that the formerly ordinary person is suddenly living in a new world with a newfound purpose.

Destined to make a difference.

Chosen.

We're drawn to these stories not because we want to leap tall buildings, wear spandex, or do whatever a spider can. (Okay, maybe a few of us do wish that.) We're drawn to these stories because the main character discovers what we've all been on a tireless search for:

- worth
- significance
- acceptance
- love
- beauty
- purpose

The biggest difference between our stories and their stories is that in real life we don't just stumble into becoming "something special." We were created that way. We were made to find our purpose, our destiny, in the One who created us. The fact that we get sidetracked, that we turn to idols to fulfill these God-given desires, doesn't change the fact that God designed us to strive for something big.

> We were made to find our purpose, our destiny, in the One who created us. The fact that we get sidetracked, that we turn to idols to fulfill these God-given desires, doesn't change the fact that God designed us to strive for something big.

This book has never been about guilt. It was never my goal to simply point out the fact that we all struggle with idolatry. Quite the opposite. I long for you to find the freedom that comes from living your life wholly seeking God. I long for you to become increasingly aware of empty promises so you won't be distracted from the Source of real power.

You need that, because the danger you face is real enough.

THE REAL ENEMY

Another key ingredient in the typical superhero drama is the hero's journey to better understand what makes his or her enemy tick—and then defeat that enemy. The hero may captivate us with courageous exploits, but he or she is nothing without a good villain. What's the point of being able to leap tall buildings in a single bound unless there's real evil to be defeated?

Similarly, a part of discovering true freedom from empty promises is understanding that there is an evil one who wants nothing more than for you to be entrapped and stuck in the vicious cycle of idolatry.

The real villain in the drama of idolatry, in other words, isn't the idols themselves. Money, possessions, productivity, beauty, and such have no real power to harm us. And our misguided hearts aren't fully to blame either.

The real villain when it comes to empty promises is the deceiver himself—Satan.

Note how he tempts Jesus in Luke 4:

> The devil led him up to a high place and showed him in an instant all the kingdoms of the world. And he said to him, "I will give you all their authority and splendor; it has been given to me, and I can give it to anyone I want to. If you worship me, it will all be yours." (vv. 5–7)

Sound familiar? Satan promised Jesus authority in the world and the splendor of riches. To us, Satan says, "I will give you . . . money, sex, power, or something else your heart desires." He swears that these things will satisfy us or make us happy—something he's incapable of delivering.

He's been saying stuff like that for a long, long time. He tempted Eve with the promise of being like God. He rolled over Job. Satan "entered" Judas before Judas sold out Jesus (Luke 22:3).

And yet we keep falling for it. Why is it that after we see person after person *not* be satisfied by empty promises, we still persist in thinking they'll make *us* happy? The carousel spins round and round, always in the same place, but we keep thinking we're on a unique journey, that this time things will be different.

Are we really that dumb? Or do we have someone speaking things to us? Tricking us? And even worse, fooling us into believing that it's not him speaking?

Why am I making such a big deal about this? Because it's so important to be clear about who our real enemy is. It's not the empty promises themselves but the one through whom they come. Satan himself is the one trying to mess us over and sell us a bill of goods.

What is it Paul says about our struggles in Ephesians 6:12? They are "not against flesh and blood, but against the rulers, against the

authorities, against the powers of this dark world and against the
spiritual forces of evil in the heavenly realms."

And these "powers of this dark world," led by Satan himself, are
not kidding around. Satan is determined to destroy us. When Peter
warned his fellow believers about Satan, what did he say? "Be alert
and of sober mind. Your enemy the devil prowls around like a roar-
ing lion looking for someone to devour" (1 Peter 5:8).

A BIBLICAL SUPERHERO

Daniel is one of the most talked-about men in the entire Bible, a
kind of biblical superhero. His story is told over and over as an
example of great courage in the face of danger, especially when
he was thrown into a pit full of hungry lions and survived. You
probably learned that story in Sunday school. But what's curiously
missing from the whole story is *any* description of Daniel's experience in that lions' den.

My friend and fellow pastor Steven Furtick pointed this out in one
of his recent blog posts, and he's absolutely right.[1] As Pastor Steven
points out, there are 153 verses describing Daniel's life before he was
thrown to the lions. Aside from a couple of verses where Daniel tells
the king that God sent an angel to shut the lions' mouths, there is no
real account of how that happened.

Think about that. A man being cast into a pit full of hungry wild
beasts makes a really interesting story. Think of all the possibilities—the teeth, the smell, the fear, the angel. Why aren't we given a
play-by-play?

I believe it's because Daniel's courage and faith in the lions' den
isn't really the point. After all, shutting the mouths of the lions was
God's thing. Once Daniel got thrown into that pit, what was he
really going to do?

I'm not saying Daniel wasn't a hero, though. What's really

impressive is the way he lived *before* he got up close and personal with those lions.

Earlier in chapter 5 we took a glance at Daniel. In this chapter I want us to look deeper into two life choices Daniel made that allowed him to avoid the land mines we call empty promises and, in so doing, be used by God in a powerful way. I believe these two choices are essential for any of us who are serious about becoming the men and women God created when he thought us into existence.

Serve Continually

We saw earlier how Daniel found favor in the eyes of King Nebuchadnezzar. Now years later a new king, King Darius, took over. Daniel continued to find favor with the king and rise in his administration. But this caused other members of the court to get jealous, so they looked for a way to bring him down:

> Now Daniel so distinguished himself among the administrators and the satraps by his exceptional qualities that the king planned to set him over the whole kingdom. At this, the administrators and the satraps tried to find grounds for charges against Daniel in his conduct of government affairs, but they were unable to do so. They could find no corruption in him, because he was trustworthy and neither corrupt nor negligent. Finally these men said, "We will never find any basis for charges against this man Daniel unless it has something to do with the law of his God." (Dan. 6:3–5)

You can imagine how frustrated those guys were. They were career politicians, accustomed to seeing corruption at every turn. But when they tried to pin some of that corruption on Daniel, they couldn't do it.

They looked for a lie he had told. Nothing.

They looked for a law he had broken. Nothing.

They looked for corners he had cut. Nothing.

They finally figured out that the only way they could catch Daniel doing something wrong was to change the rules. So they went to King Darius, buttered him up, and talked him into creating a law that would interfere with Daniel's famous devotion to God. The new law stated that for the next thirty days no one could pray to any god or human except the king himself.

> Now when Daniel learned that the decree had been published, he went home to his upstairs room where the windows opened toward Jerusalem. Three times a day he got down on his knees and prayed, giving thanks to his God, just as he had done before. Then these men went as a group and found Daniel praying and asking God for help. So they went to the king and spoke to him about his royal decree: "Did you not publish a decree that during the next thirty days anyone who prays to any god or human being except to you, Your Majesty, would be thrown into the lions' den?" (vv. 10–12)

Why did that group of advisors know that Daniel's faith was the way to trap him? Because they had seen that faith lived out on a daily basis.

There is a great phrase that appears several times in the book of Daniel. The Babylonians used it to describe what they saw happening between Daniel and his God, the kind of relationship they saw in Daniel's life. They talked about the God "whom you serve *continually*" (Dan. 6:16 and 6:20).

Not occasionally.

Not sporadically.

Not when it's convenient.

The God whom you serve *continually*.

I think most people want a lions'-den experience where God

does huge things in their lives. A moment when God comes through for them in big ways.

But most people will never have the opportunity to prove God's faithfulness in the lions' den because they have not established their faith in everyday life.

They're not going to see God come through for them in a huge way financially because they haven't learned to trust him with 10 percent of what they have.

They're not going to see increased favor at work because they segregate God from their work.

They're not going to see God use them in powerful ways at school because they live in such a way that no one there knows they even believe in God.

> I don't think being mature Christians means getting to a place where we never deal with idolatry. Rather, maturity comes when we become aware that this is going to be a lifelong battle . . . and we make up our minds to engage in it on a daily basis.

The key to living a heroic Christian life isn't trying to be like the Daniel in the lions' den. It's being like the Daniel who prayed every day and held on to his integrity. It's being like the Daniel who served God continually, who constantly and consistently fought against the quick fix that often accompanies the temptation of idolatry.

I don't think being mature Christians means getting to a place where we never deal with idolatry. Rather, maturity comes when we become aware that this is going to be a lifelong battle . . . and we make up our minds to engage in it on a daily basis. It's this realization, I believe, that puts us on the road to freedom from the empty promises that attempt to control us.

Believe Endlessly

Not only did Daniel serve continually; he also believed endlessly. And it probably wasn't an easy thing to do.

The man endured a lot in his life. From his childhood on, he experienced numerous events that could have caused him to give up his faith and devotion to God. And I suspect there were years of unanswered prayers that made Daniel feel as if God had forgotten him or, maybe even worse, that God didn't care.

He must have prayed when he was a kid and Babylon was rising as a world power. When Nebuchadnezzar threatened the little country of Israel, Daniel must have prayed Nebuchadnezzar wouldn't defeat them. But Nebuchadnezzar won.

When Babylon took some of the brightest and the best young people from Israel into captivity, Daniel must have prayed he would not be among them. But he was one of those teenagers who had to make the long march to the Babylonian king's palace.

Then years later, when Daniel heard about the new decree where everyone had to pray to King Darius, he must have prayed King Darius would change his mind about the decree, that it would not be enforced. Unfortunately, that didn't happen either.

I'm not saying that Daniel never experienced the faithfulness of God. In fact, he felt God's touch again and again in his life. But there were also periods when everything seemed to be going wrong and God seemed far away. In those times, it couldn't have been an easy thing for Daniel to keep on believing.

You know, if I'm honest, I am far more prone to start searching for a false god when I cannot sense the presence of the real God— or when it seems as though he's let me down. Isn't this often the catalyst for idolatry in our lives?

Just go back to one of the first biblical examples of idolatry in the Bible—the same one we looked at in chapter 1. Moses had led the Israelites out of Egypt, remember, but then had disappeared for an extended time. He was getting the Ten Commandments, but the Israelites didn't know that. So they talked Aaron into making a golden idol for them to worship.

In their minds, a present leader represented a present God. Though God had never left them, not even for a second, they perceived otherwise. They were willing to turn to a false god, a golden calf that absolutely couldn't offer them anything more than just existing. It couldn't speak, breathe, lead, or perform the miraculous, but by golly it was there in their midst. And to the Israelites, who felt abandoned, that was a big temptation to idolatry.

And we're not so different, you and I. It's in those times that God seems distant that our idols seem especially appealing. After all, they're available.

We can call them.

We can eat them or drink them or smoke them. Well, some of them.

We can manipulate them.

We can buy and sell them.

We can use them as distractions from what we really need.

We're willing to sell out to these idols because we don't want to depend on a God that's invisible and at times difficult to sense. Holding on to belief in times like that just seems too difficult.

With so many of Daniel's prayers seemingly unanswered, he was the perfect candidate to jump headfirst into idolatry. But he didn't. Instead, he continued to believe. And as he was thrown into the lions' den he must have prayed once again, "God, please save me."

And this one God did answer.

I love the interchange that happens between Daniel and King Darius the morning after Daniel was thrown into the lions' den.

At the first light of dawn, the king got up and hurried to the lions' den. When he came near the den, he called to Daniel in an anguished voice, "Daniel, servant of the living God, has your God, whom you serve continually, been able to rescue you from the lions?"

Daniel answered, "May the king live forever! My God sent his angel, and he shut the mouths of the lions. They have not hurt me, because I was found innocent in his sight. Nor have I ever done any wrong before you, Your Majesty. (vv. 19–22)

And Daniel's stubborn belief didn't just lead to a miraculous work in his own life. His faith squashed idolatry in the lives of other people. His trust in God allowed other people to see the emptiness of the things they were trusting in. Look how King Darius responded.

I issue a decree that in every part of my kingdom people must fear and reverence the God of Daniel.

> *For he is the living God*
> *and he endures forever;*
> *his kingdom will not be destroyed,*
> *his dominion will never end.*
> *He rescues and he saves;*
> *he performs signs and wonders*
> *in the heavens and on the earth.*
> *He has rescued Daniel*
> *from the power of the lions. (vv. 26–27)*

As Daniel heard these words rolling off the tongue of King Darius, he must have thought, *Yep, that's my God. You can serve any God you want. You can pray to any God you want, but there is only one God who is able.*

THE REAL THING

I want you to know that I believe with all my heart that our God is able to meet our deepest needs. He is not a myth. He is not an abstraction or a lovely idea. He's not the latest trend.

There are very few neutral moments in life. Each and every one offers an opportunity, a choice, to either draw closer to the likeness and presence of our Creator or to drift further away by falling for the empty promises of this world. . . . Every moment of every day offers us the opportunity to be drawn into God's presence, be shaped by his grace, and take a step toward home.

He is real. He made everything that is. He stands above time, space, and history. What seems impossible to me isn't remotely difficult for him.

He's not an empty promise, in other words. He's the real thing.

That means you don't have to live in fear.

You don't have to live in defeat or search for something, anything, to heal the hurt or fill the empty places in your life, because our God is able to do all that.

He is able to reconcile a broken marriage.

He is able to liberate people from horrible addictions.

He is able to forgive the darkest of sins and make somebody into a new creature.

He is able to provide for the most pressing need.

He is able to guide with supernatural wisdom.

Our God is able.

And he is exactly what you've been searching for your whole life. You've looked for it from the approval of your parents.

You've tried to find it by achieving greater and greater things.

But it was right here all along. Right here in God, your Creator. For he, and he alone, can give you what none of these other counterfeit gods could ever give you.

ONLY HOME WILL DO

When I was a kid I used to attend a church camp called Happy Hill Acres. My week at Happy Hill Acres was unlike any other week of the year.

There were no nice living quarters. We stayed in rustic cabins full of bunk beds.

There was no television, so we had to learn to enjoy the simpler entertainment like shuffleboard, Uno, and foosball.

There was no air conditioning.

Thinking back, there really wasn't a whole lot happy about Happy Hill Acres.

Though I attended the summer camp for years I'll never forget the summer I turned nine. I was horribly homesick that week. Every night I would bury myself deep into my sleeping bag so the other kids wouldn't hear me crying myself to sleep.

I tried to forget about home by jumping headfirst into every activity the camp offered. But nothing worked. I missed home so badly. I was miserable. I had an inconsolable void in me that could only be filled by going home.

Camp ended on Saturday, but on Wednesday I faked sick and got sent home early. I can't tell you how excited I was when I saw my parents drive up to get me. I knew without a doubt that the only thing that would take my pain away was home.

This is an important reality we have to address as we begin to wrap up the subject of idols and empty promises. In this life, no matter how hard we seek God and God alone, no matter how continually we serve and how endlessly we believe, there will still be a tinge of emptiness deep within our souls. While seeking God and God alone certainly brings purpose, satisfaction, and value to our lives, we still won't feel complete, at least not all the time.

Why?

We're not supposed to. We're not home yet.

No relationship with God in this present world will ever be as rich, fulfilling, or freeing as it will be in heaven.

I think we've done a disservice in our churches by saying God can provide us with a completely satisfying life, but not adding that this won't happen completely in our lifetimes. We're not helping people if we don't warn them of what I call the "inconsolable emptiness" of life on earth.

C. S. Lewis wrote, "If I find in myself a desire which no experience in this world can satisfy, the most probable explanation is that I was made for another world."[2]

I think we often miss this. We think what we want is a bigger title, better looks, more popularity, larger sums of money, the perfect spouse. However, what we really want is the person we were made for—Jesus—and the place we were made for—heaven.

But this doesn't mean we should just give up. Either we point our inner emptiness toward God, trusting him for our eventual fulfillment, or we can make the decision to fend for ourselves and turn to empty promises that only make that inner emptiness worse.

There are very few neutral moments in life. Each and every one offers an opportunity, a choice, to either draw closer to the likeness and presence of our Creator or to drift further away by falling for the empty promises of this world.

This idea shouldn't scare us, guilt us, or paralyze us. We shouldn't go crazy over it but simply approach it in a freeing way, realizing that every moment of every day offers us the opportunity to be drawn into God's presence, be shaped by his grace, and take a step toward home. Our lives can literally be transformed when we choose to live in the constant awareness of God's presence.

One of the greatest themes of Scripture is God's constant, repetitive communication of "I am with you. Now, will you be with me?"

The rainbow was God saying to Noah, "I am with you. Will you choose to be with me?"

The birth of Isaac was God's way of saying to Abraham, "I am with you. Will you choose to be with me?"

The provision of manna was God saying to the Israelites, "I am with you. Will you choose to be with me?"

The Jordan River piling up in a heap, the sound of Goliath hitting the ground, the bull being consumed by fire, the king's edict protecting the Jews—all those were variations of the same message from God: "I am with you. Will you choose to be with me?"

And the birth of Emmanuel—Jesus? That was God saying to the whole world, "I am with you. Will you choose to be with me?"

The cross and the empty tomb was God saying it with a megaphone: "I am with you. Will you choose to be with me?"

And it goes on—with the Holy Spirit bursting onto the scene in Acts 2, the violent earthquake shaking the prison cell in Acts 16, John's revelation on the island of Patmos. Again and again in Scripture, we have that promise that if we draw near to God, he will draw near to us (James 4:8).

John Ortberg wrote, "At the end of the day, we do not have a program, plan, platform, or product to help the world. We have a savior. We do not point to success, knowledge, pleasure, or power. We point to a cross."[3]

The cross is more than the starting line of our faith. It is what our faith orbits around. And it's in the shadow of that cross that I pray you'll never settle for anything less than the person God created you to be.

I pray the cross will be a reminder to you that Jesus didn't just defeat the consequences of sin, allowing you the possibility of eternity with him. He also defeated the power of sin, making transformation available in this life as well. For it is as we turn from empty promises to his real presence that we are changed:

- from driven to dedicated;
- from needy to affirmed;
- from controlling to surrendered;
- from greedy to giving;
- from ruled by religion to free in faith;
- from appearance-obsessed to truly beautiful;
- from frustrated with the past to trusting for the future.

If we can learn to find our ultimate satisfaction in God from one moment to the next moment to the next, we can make sure our lives count for what matters most and enjoy the very best God has to offer. And we'll never be the same.

> The cross is more than the starting line of our faith. It is what our faith orbits around. And it's in the shadow of that cross that I pray you'll never settle for anything less than the person God created you to be.

The people around us will never be the same.

This world will never be the same.

Even while we're haunted by the inconsolable emptiness of knowing we're not home yet, we can still experience true, fulfilling satisfaction an idol could never provide. Tomorrow will soon be upon us, and we'll all be faced with an incredible invitation from Jesus to worship him "in spirit and in truth" (John 4:23 NLT).

Listen! Do you hear it? Jesus is calling you to give up your idols and put all your trust in him. For he alone is worthy of your whole devotion.

He alone has the authority to forgive all your sins.

He alone has the wisdom to guide your whole life.

He alone has the power to fill your gnawing inner emptiness.

And Jesus alone has the power to bring you home, one day, to where you belong—with him.

Because that's been your destiny all along.

NOTES

Chapter One: Deceptively Good

1. John Calvin, *Institutes of the Christian Religion*, 1.11.8, quoted in Nick Nowalk, "Smashing Idols," *The Harvard Ichthus: A Journal of Christian Thought and Expression*, http://www.harvardichthus.org/fishtank/2010/03/smashing-our-idols/.
2. C. S. Lewis, *Mere Christianity* (New York: HarperCollins, 2001), 135.
3. Lewis Smedes, *Standing on the Promises: Keeping Hope Alive for a Tomorrow We Cannot Control* (Nashville: Thomas Nelson, 1998), 41.

Chapter Two: The Aware Life

1. Ruth Haley Barton, *Sacred Rhythms: Arranging Our Lives for Spiritual Transformation* (Downers Grove, IL: InterVarsity, 2006), 94, italics mine.
2. Dallas Willard, quoted in John Ortberg, "Tiger and the Good Life: Celebrities and Obituaries Offer Competing Definitions of What's Worth Pursuing," *Leadership Journal* (online edition), December 14, 2009, http://www.christianitytoday.com/le/currenttrendscolumns/leadershipweekly/tigerandthegoodlife.html. Originally offered in "Character and Curriculum: The Impact of Classroom Content on Spiritual Formation," Key Issues Session presented at the International Forum on Christian Higher Education, May 31, 2006, transcript available online at http://www.dwillard.org/resources/CCCU2006c.asp.

3. C. S. Lewis, *The Weight of Glory* (New York: Harper Collins, 2001), 26.

Chapter Three: The Seduction of Achievement

1. Some details of this letter, including names, have been changed.
2. Erwin Raphael McManus, "Driven, Destined, and Determined to Change," in *Soul Cravings* (Nashville: Thomas Nelson, 2006), Destiny Entry 18.
3. Quoted in Lynn Hirschberg, "The Misfit," *Vanity Fair*, April 1991, 160–69, 196–202, quoted in Timothy Keller, *Counterfeit Gods: The Empty Promises of Money, Sex, and Power, and the Only Hope That Matters* (New York: Dutton, 1998), 72.
4. Harriet Rubin, "Success and Excess," *Fast Company*, September 30, 1998, http://www.fastcompany.com/magazine/18/success.html?page=0%2C2.

Chapter Four: Addicted to Approval

1. Henri Nouwen, *Clowning in Rome: Reflections on Solitude, Celibacy, Prayer, and Contemplation* (New York: Doubleday Image, 1979), 39.
2. Timothy Keller, *Counterfeit Gods: The Empty Promises of Money, Sex, and Power, and the Only Hope That Matters* (New York: Dutton, 1998), 37. The commentator referred to in this selection is Derek Kidner, *Genesis: An Introduction and Commentary* (Downers Grove, IL: InterVarsity, 1967), 160.
3. Erwin Raphael McManus, "Being Loved to Death?" in *Soul Cravings* (Nashville: Thomas Nelson, 2006), Intimacy Entry 13.

Chapter Five: The Perils of Power

1. C. S. Lewis, *God in the Dock* (Grand Rapids: Eerdmans, 2001), 56.
2. Jeffrey Pfeffer, *Power: Why Some People Have It—and Others Don't* (New York: HarperCollins, 2010), 195.
3. Timothy Keller, *Counterfeit Gods: The Empty Promises of Money, Sex, and Power, and the Only Hope That Matters* (New York: Dutton, 1998), 121.

Chapter Six: Money Always Wants to Be More than Money

1. Graeme Wood, "Secret Fears of the Super-Rich," *The Atlantic*, April 2011, http://www.theatlantic.com/magazine/archive/2011/04/secret-fears-of-the-super-rich/8419/.
2. Brent Kessel, "How Much Money Is Enough?" MSN Money, July 14, 2008, http://articles.moneycentral.msn.com/Investing/StockInvestingTrading/HowMuchMoneyIsEnough.aspx.
3. Max Lucado, *Traveling Light: Releasing the Burdens You Were Never Intended to Bear: The Promise of Psalm 23*, library ed. (Nashville: Thomas Nelson, 2001), 29
4. Judith Warner, "The Charitable-Giving Divide," *New York Times Magazine*, August 20, 2010, http://www.nytimes.com/2010/08/22/magazine/22FOB-wwln-t.html. See also John Stossel and Kristina Kendall, "Who Gives and

Who Doesn't?" *20/20*, November 28, 2006, http://abcnews.go.com/2020
/story?id=2682730&page=1.

Chapter Seven: Religion Lies

1. William J. Larkin Jr., *Acts*, The IVP New Testament Commentary Series
   (Downers Grove, IL: InterVarsity, 1995), accessed on BibleGateway.com as
   "Acts 8—IVP New Testament Commentaries," http://www.biblegateway
   .com/resources/commentaries/IVP-NT/Acts/Philip-Ethiopian-Eunuch.
2. David Crowder, "Sometimes," © 2011 sixsteps Music / worshiptogether.com
   Songs /Inot Music (Admin. at EMICMGPublishing.com) (ASCAP). You can
   listen to this wonderful song and find links for downloading at http://www
   .worshiptogether.com/songs/songdetail.aspx?iid=1836139.

Chapter Eight: Addicted to Beauty

1. Shaun Dreisbach, "Shocking Body-Image News: 97% of Women Will Be
   Cruel to Their Bodies Today," *Glamour*, February 2011, http://www
   .glamour.com/health-fitness/2011/02/shocking-body-image-news-97
   -percent-of-women-will-be-cruel-to-their-bodies-today.
2. Ibid.
3. Sarah Knapton, "Solid Gold Statue of Kate Moss Unveiled at British
   Museum," *Telegraph*, August 28, 2008, http://www.telegraph.co.uk/news
   /celebritynews/2636358/Solid-gold-statue-of-Kate-Moss-unveiled-at-British
   -Museum.html.
4. Michelle Graham, *Wanting to Be Her: Body Image Secrets Victoria Won't Tell You*
   (Downers Grove, IL: InterVarsity, 2005), 14–15.
5. For a quick summary of some of the factors thought to affect the
   development of anorexia nervosa, see Roxanne Dryden-Edwards, "Anorexia
   Nervosa," MedicineNet.com, http://www.medicinenet.com/anorexia
   _nervosa/article.htm#tocd.
6. Katy Lee, "Competitive Beauty Pageant Prompts Mom to Use Botox on Her
   Daughter," Walnut Patch, May 17, 2011, http://walnut.patch.com/articles
   /competitive-beauty-pageant-prompts-mom-to-use-botox-on-her-daughter.
7. Michelle Myers, *The Look That Kills: An Anorexic's Addiction to Control*
   (Nashville: CrossBooks, 2010), 33.
8. Ibid., 95.
9. Margery Williams, *The Velveteen Rabbit or How Toys Become Real* (NY: Avon,
   1975, first published 1922), 12–13.

Chapter Nine: Chasing a Dream

1. Dallas Willard, "The Gospel of the Kingdom and Spiritual Formation," in
   The Kingdom Life: A Practical Theology of Discipleship and Spiritual Formation,
   ed. Alan Andrews (Colorado Springs: NavPress, 2010), 41.

Chapter Ten: You Are What You Worship

1. John Ortberg, "Kings and Priests," catalystspace, January 11, 2011, http://www
.catalystspace.com/content/read/article_JAN11--kings_and_priests--ortberg/.
2. Carolyn Custis James, *Half the Church: Recapturing God's Global Vision for
Women* (Grand Rapids: Zondervan, 2010), 54, 56.
3. N. T. Wright, quoted in Ortberg, "Kings and Priests."
4. Ibid.
5. A. W. Tozer, *The Knowledge of the Holy* (New York: HarperCollins, 1961), 1.
6. Richard J. Foster, *Celebration of Discipline: The Path to Spiritual Growth*, 3rd ed.
(New York: HarperCollins, 1998), 171–72.

Chapter Eleven: Living Close to Truth

1. Dallas Willard, *The Spirit of Disciplines: Understanding How God Changes Lives*
(New York: HarperCollins, 1991), 163.
2. Henri Nouwen, *The Way of the Heart: Desert Spirituality and Contemporary
Ministry* (New York: Harper Collins, 1991), 27–28.
3. John Piper, *A Hunger for God: Desiring God Through Fasting and Prayer*
(Wheaton, IL: Crossway, 1997), 14.
4. Richard J.Foster, *Celebration of Discipline: The Path to Spiritual Growth*, 3rd ed.
(New York: Harper Collins, 1998), 55.
5. William C. Taylor, "Permission Marketing," *Fast Company*, March 31, 1998,
http://www.fastcompany.com/magazine/14/permission.html. See also
Lonny Kocina, "The Average American Is Exposed to . . ." Publicity.com,
http://www.publicity.com/articles/the-average-american-is-exposed-to-/.
6. John Ortberg, *The Me I Want to Be: Becoming God's Best Version of You* (Grand
Rapids: Zondervan, 2010), 136.
7. Ibid., 134.
8. Henri Nouwen, *Clowning in Rome: Reflections on Solitude, Celibacy, Prayer, and
Contemplation* (New York: Doubleday Image, 1979), 60.

Chapter Twelve: Soul Satisfaction

1. Steven Furtick, "Real Courage," Steven Furtick, January 13, 2011, http://
www.stevenfurtick.com/spiritual-growth/real-courage/.
2. C. S. Lewis, *Mere Christianity* (New York: HarperCollins, 2001), 136–37.
3. John Ortberg, *The Me I Want to Be: Becoming God's Best Version of You* (Grand
Rapids: Zondervan, 2010), 253.